LOCAL GOVERNMENT REORGANISATION

Of related interest

QUANGOS AND LOCAL GOVERNMENT
A Changing World
Edited by Howard Davis

FINANCING EUROPEAN LOCAL GOVERNMENTS
Edited by John Gibson and Richard Batley

THE POLITICAL EXECUTIVE
Politicians and Management in European Local Government
Edited by Richard Batley and Adrian Campbell

POLITICS IN AUSTRIA
Edited by Dr Richard Luther and Dr Wolfgang C. Muller

PARLIAMENTS IN WESTERN EUROPE
Edited by Philip Norton

THE POLITICS OF THE NETHERLANDS
HOW MUCH CHANGE?
Edited by Hans Daadler and Galen A. Irwin

UNDERSTANDING THE SWEDISH MODEL
Edited by Jan-Erik Lane

Local Government Reorganisation:
The Review and its Aftermath

Edited by

STEVE LEACH

Routledge
Taylor & Francis Group

LONDON AND NEW YORK

First published in 1998 in Great Britain by
FRANK CASS AND COMPANY LIMITED

2 Park Square, Milton Park, Abingdon, Oxfordshire OX14 4RN
711 Third Avenue, New York, NY 10017

Routledge is an imprint of the Taylor and Francis Group, an informa business

First issued in paperback 2015

Copyright © 1998 Frank Cass & Co. Ltd

British Library Cataloguing in Publication Data

Local government reorganisation: The review and its aftermath.
    1. Local government – Great Britain. 2. Legislative bodies –
Great Britain – Reform
I. Leach, Steve
352.2'214'0941

Library of Congress Cataloging-in-Publication Data

Local government reorganisation: The review and its aftermath /
edited by
    Steve Leach.
        p. cm.
    "This group of studies first appeared in a special issue of Local
government studies, vol. 23, no. 3 (Autumn 1997)" – T.p. verso.
Includes bibliographical references and index.
    ISBN 978-0-7146-4859-0 (hbk)
    ISBN 978-1-138-99550-5 (pbk)
    1. Local government–Great Britain. I. Leach, Steve.
JS3111.P47 1997
320.8–dc21   97-29368
                                              CIP

This group of studies first appeared in a Special Issue of
Local Government Studies, Vol.23, No.3 (Autumn 1997),
[Local Government Reorganisation: The Review and its Aftermath].

Contents

Introduction:
The Continuing Relevance of the Local Government Review

STEVE LEACH

The Local Government Review (LGR) in England has not, by and large, been a rewarding or happy experience for the majority of authorities who were drawn into it. Although those authorities which have achieved unitary status are generally positive about the outcome (if not always about the process which led up to it), elsewhere the Review has generated a good deal of frustration, loss of morale and a sense of injustice. Districts who still feel that *their* case for unitary status is just as strong as many of the 46 new authorities that have been (or are soon to be) established, and counties who are preparing for (or trying to cope with) the loss of one (or more) districts which have been central to their service strategies and strategic concerns have perhaps been particularly affected by these reactions. But even in counties where there has been no change and no strong case for change perceived by the Local Government Commission (LGC) or (ultimately) the previous government, there remains a sense of expectations raised and then time and staff resources wasted on a process which proved to have little consistency, logic or direction to it.

Such reactions will take time to dissipate; indeed it is not unlikely that attempts will be made to resurrect the idea of a further reorganisation. Such a development would be a total anathema, I suspect, to the vast majority of authorities, who are still recovering from the effects of the last Review. For many authorities the priority must be to draw a thick black line under the whole bizarre process. That response merits a good deal of empathy.

In such circumstances the question might be raised of how a study on the subject of the Local Government Review can be justified, especially in the light of the recent publication of a special issue of *Public Administration* on the same topic[1] (in which the editor of this volume was also involved).

The main justification is the way in which the LGR provides such an invaluable learning opportunity for academics and practitioners alike. It is important to make the most of that opportunity, whilst the experience

Steve Leach, De Montfort University.

remains reasonably fresh in the minds of those involved, as willing or unwilling participants, or as academic onlookers. It is only now the Review is over[2] that it is possible to interpret the process (with the benefit of hindsight) in a holistic way. The advantages of so doing are recognised even by those who have been critical of the process and whose authorities have suffered unwanted change. As John Sinnott rightly argues[3]

> The local government review was an inept exercise, but shameless as much as shameful. Even the poll tax produced an admission of error. If not now, when will the local government review produce the same? *If the lessons are not learnt, the only loser will be local government itself.* (my italics)

The Review is of particular interest to academics because it raises so many fascinating issues of political process and provides a test-bed for a range of decision-making theories (see below). The interest for practitioners, in addition to the insights provided by academic analysis, lies in the highlighting of the lessons to be learned. If there is to be a further review in the foreseeable future – and the instability and logical inconsistency of the outcome of the Review in England certainly raises that possibility[4] – then it *must* be done better than it was last time. That surely is a principle on which all can agree!

In this volume we have attempted to respond to both these perspectives. In relation to academic analysis, there are a series of articles, all with policy relevance, which examine different aspects of the review process. Howard Davis provides an overview of the English Review, highlighting the key events and changes of direction, in a way which makes for an interesting comparison with other recent attempts to carry out similar retrospective analyses.[5] Steve Leach examines the LGR in terms of policy process, arguing that because the process (in England at least) was undertaken by a Commission, certain expectations of 'rational analysis' were raised, only to be disappointed. The garbage-can model of policy process[6] provides in many ways a more convincing perspective, with 'problems' and 'solutions' chasing one another throughout the process.

The LGR was instigated by a Conservative government which had by the time of the policy launch (1991) already implemented a profound programme of changes in local government, many of which can be seen as components of what has became known as the 'new managerialism'.[7] It was widely expected that the LGR would reflect this perspective, together with other related concepts, such as 'enabling' and 'consumerism'. Bob Leach and Neil Barnett show how initial attempts to steer the Review in this direction were never sustained, and the opportunity to apply what was by then a well-established set of ideological principles to a territorial review was lost.

A second interesting basis for testing the outcomes of the Local Government Review can be developed from the precepts of 'public choice theory', which has been argued to underpin many of the Conservative government's public service reforms. George Boyne examines the outcomes of the review process in Scotland and Wales against a number of criteria developed from public choice theory. He concludes that 'despite the aura of economic logic which surrounds public choice theory, it does not deliver a "rational plan" for "local government structure from first principles"'.[8]

The most fruitful locations for an assessment of the implementation challenges and problems of a switch from a two-tier system to a structure based on unitary authorities are provided by Scotland and Wales, both of which experienced a comprehensive reorganisation of this nature in April 1996. Arthur Midwinter and Neil McGarvey examines the way in which the transition was managed in Scotland, arguing that this process was largely successful, but that some interesting (and perhaps unexpected) issues of 'patronage politics' emerged during the process.

Two contrasting practitioner perspectives are provided in the contributions by John Sinnott, Chief Executive of Leicestershire CC, and Tim Mobbs, Head of Central Services in South Norfolk. South Norfolk DC was one of the (many) unsuccessful applicants for unitary status, Leicestershire CC one of the many counties which now have to operate in a 'hybrid' system with two of the previous districts having been granted unitary status, one (the City of Leicester) right in the centre of the county area. Both authors are critical of particular aspects of the review process. Both stress the importance of learning from the mistakes involved.

Finally, Don Norris comments on the English review process on the basis of USA perspectives and experiences, arguing that the legal and cultural traditions in the USA would make local government reorganisations of the kind experienced here impossible there.

The Local Government Review may be over for the time being at least. But it leaves in its wake a whole range of unresolved dilemmas and unanswered questions. This special issue has been drawn up with the aims of providing at least some clarification of and insight into a strange and complex process, and of emphasising the lessons to be learned.

NOTES

1. Steve Leach and Gerry Stoker (eds.), *The Local Government Review in England 1991–96*, Special Issue of *Public Administration*, Vol.75, No.1 (Spring 1997).
2. Disregarding the not inconsiderable problems of the implementation of change in the 19 unitary authorities which will be established in April 1998.
3. John Sinnott, 'The Local Government Review: An Inept Process', see this volume, pp. 90–107.
4. S. Leach and G. Stoker, 'Understanding The Local Government Review: A Retrospective

Analysis', *Public Administration*, op. cit., pp.17–18.
5. See Leach and Stoker, op. cit.; and G. Wendt, *The Last Word? Reflections on the Local Government Review* (London: Association of County Councils, 1997).
6. See M. Cohen, James March and J. Ulsen, 'A Garbage Can Model of Organisational Choice', *Administrative Science Quarterly*, Vol.17 (1992), pp.1–25.
7. See Vivien Lowndes, 'Change in Public Service Management: New Institutions and New Managerial Regimes', *Local Government Studies*, Vol.23, No.2 (1997).
8. George Boyne, 'Public Choice Theory and Local Government Structure', see this volume, pp.56–72.

Reviewing the Review

HOWARD DAVIS

The election of a Labour government in May 1997 may in time come to be seen as the point at which the English local government review (LGR) process was re-opened. The new government has a massive agenda of constitutional change, much of which will have a significant impact on local government. Proposals range from a commitment to signing the European Charter of Local Self Government (giving UK local government, for the first time, something amounting to the beginnings of constitutional protection), through to an examination of electoral reform. In addition, although the term is not used, Britain may be on the verge of beginning the process of converting itself into a federal country.

Subject to referenda confirming popular support, the government proposes the creation of a Scottish 'parliament with law-making powers'[1] (the first since 1707) and a Welsh 'assembly' with 'secondary legislative powers'.[2] In England Labour had previously indicated its criticism of the Conservative government's 'reluctance to develop a rational structure for England's regions'.[3] Its general election manifesto sets out a commitment to establish 'regional chambers'[4] to co-ordinate bids for European funding, economic development strategy, transport and strategic land-use planning. 'In time' legislation will be introduced to allow the people 'region by region' to decide by referendum whether they wish to convert these regional chambers into directly elected 'regional assemblies'. The government takes the view that the creation of elected regional assemblies 'would require a predominantly unitary system of local government' as 'our plans will not mean adding a new tier of government to the existing English system'.[5] The change will also require confirmation by independent auditors that, overall, no additional public expenditure will be involved. There is a slight change of wording from Labour's 1995 consultation paper on its plans for England's regions, which had said: 'A precondition [of the change] would be the establishment of a basically unitary system of local government',[6] although this does not seem to be of any major significance. London will, subject to popular consent, move straight to a directly elected 'strategic authority'[7] and mayor without the intervening stage of a regional chamber.

Howard Davis, Inlogov, University of Birmingham.

The appointment of Deputy Prime Minister John Prescott as Secretary of State for the Environment, Transport and the Regions is a signal of the importance of the regional question to the new government. Local government reorganisation is thus back on the political agenda when many may have thought the issue closed. Labour's 1995 consultation paper set out the process that the party had in mind for triggering the move to a directly elected regional assembly.[8] The first stage would be for the regional chamber, by resolution, to propose a plan for the change – importantly to include 'arrangements for unitary authorities',[9] the boundaries of which would be subject to the agreement of the Secretary of State after consultation with the opposition parties. Parliamentary orders to confirm the plan would then be required before the holding of a referendum. If this process is adhered to it presages some interesting debates and battles in the next stage of the revived LGR.

The membership of the regional chambers which have to produce the reorganisation proposals will be from the existing local authorities in the region. The government therefore cleverly passes the poisoned chalice of local government reorganisation to local government itself! Labour has previously said that it wishes the regional chambers to be given the chance to 'establish themselves properly over a reasonable period of time'[10] and that the timescale for moving from regional chambers to regional assemblies 'is bound to vary from one region to another'.[11] Indeed, 'There may be some areas which do not want to make this move at all. We anticipate that there will be strong pressure for this move in the north, north-west and south-west, but perhaps less immediate pressure elsewhere'.[12] The story could be particularly interesting in the Yorkshire and Humberside region. That region contains North, South and West Yorkshire along with Humberside. Humberside, South Yorkshire, West Yorkshire and the City of York already have unitary local government. Only North Yorkshire (outside York itself) still retains a two-tier local government system. The votes in that region would seem to be stacked against North Yorkshire before the process begins! The longevity of its current system of local government must therefore be in considerable doubt.

It is also, of course, open to the government to use the powers of the Local Government Act 1992 to direct the Local Government Commission for England (LGCE) to carry out further structural reviews of defined areas. For instance, the new government may well act on the former (Conservative) Secretary of State's letter to the Chairman of the LGCE that he expected 'it will not be very long' before the Commission received a direction to conduct a further review (the third) of Northampton.[13] Indeed, some 20 shire districts who believe strongly in unitary local government have recently formed a 'Local Governance Review Group' to campaign for the government to complete the 'unfinished business' of the LGR. The 'direction option' may be particularly relevant in regions of traditional Conservative strength if, as might be expected, the Conservatives manage to rebuild a local government base over the coming years. If no regional consensus can be built for the comprehensive reorganisation of local government then certain (mainly Labour) districts are likely to press the government to use the alternative route of a further LGCE review.

The spectre of instability is thus raised once again as authorities begin to look into the future. County councils are often thought to be the most vulnerable, with their responsibilities passing both up (to the regions) and down (to the new unitaries). However, existing shire districts cannot be assumed to be 'safe', and even metropolitan districts, and the shire unitaries created so far, could get caught up in a review if a wider regional view is being taken. It is, therefore, worth looking at the LGR so far to see what lessons can be learned.

BACKGROUND TO THE LGR

In its early days the LGR had been presented by Michael Heseltine, then Secretary of State for the Environment, as 'an opportunity to think afresh about the structure of local authorities' whilst adopting 'a practical approach in response to local views and local conditions'.[14] There had long been rumblings of discontent about the outcome of the 1974 reorganisation of local government. Furthermore, abolition of the Greater London Council and the six metropolitan county councils in 1986 had left clear anomalies. For example, Bristol, with a population of almost 400,000, had the restricted functions of a shire district whilst Kingston-upon-Thames, with a population of less than 150,000, had become the focus of most local government functions within its area.

However, it was the poll tax, the political difficulties that it caused and the Conservative leadership election arising from that situation that proved to be the impetus for setting the LGR in train. Withdrawal from the poll tax needed a tactical retreat and part of that process, initiated by Michael Heseltine, was to look at local government in the round – not just the way it was financed, but also its structure and internal management. In addition, the erosion of local government powers and of local government's role as a direct provider of services began to raise questions as to whether sufficient work remained for two tiers of principal authorities.

The concept of a single tier of elected local authorities (unitary authorities) had a simplistic allure. With only one tier it was thought that the visibility of local government would increase and public confusion as to who did what would decrease. Accountability would be increased because it would be clear where 'the buck stopped'. Also for those, such as Michael Heseltine, who wished to see local government radically transform its internal management, unitary local authorities were seen to fit more readily with concepts such as directly elected mayors.

A reorganisation of local government also offered some populist and nostalgic opportunities. Some of the authorities and amalgamations which dated from 1974 'but which have not succeeded in inspiring local loyalty'[15] could be undone. County areas such as Humberside and Hereford & Worcester can be seen in this category. In addition, many areas which had long histories of local self-government but had seen their status reduced in 1974 could have that status restored. This included a few historic counties (for example, Rutland) and many former county boroughs which, prior to 1974, had, in local government terms, been independent of their surrounding counties (for example, Nottingham, Portsmouth).

The possibility of unitary local authorities also had attractions for the then opposition, the Labour Party in particular. Many of the areas that had lost status in 1974 had a history of Labour control. That reorganisation had in most cases subordinated those areas to county councils which were at best 'hung' (that is, no single political party had overall control) and at worst (at least until the 1993 county council elections) Conservative-controlled. Labour politics have always had a strong parochial streak and this loss of the ability to dominate the local agenda in some communities (because the county council was now a key player) was often bitterly resented.

In addition, Labour has long had a commitment to some form of regional government, as the programme of the new government shows. For many advocates of regional government unitary local authorities are a necessary part of the process. Without a unitary structure, it is argued, England would be over-governed. Local government reorganisation is therefore seen to be a necessary prerequisite *en route* to the regional goal.

The omens, therefore, might have seemed good. A senior government minister was committed to driving the policy forward. The review tapped into a number of long-standing concerns, including those of the then opposition, and it offered some populist opportunities into the bargain. The devil, however, was in the detail. At the level of a general idea propositions can often seem attractive. However, once the details begin to be worked out the practical implications for areas, institutions and individuals begin to be identified. Support for the general idea can turn into opposition against proposals for its implementation. That was exactly what happened in many parts of England. As authorities and local politicians looked into the future, and found that the perceived benefits were not going to flow to them, initial positions often changed.

THE REVIEW BEGINS

In April 1991 a Conservative government consultation paper expressed the view that there should be 'a move towards unitary authorities where these do not already exist',[16] but also indicated an apparent open-mindedness: 'The aim will be to achieve the structure which best matches the particular circumstances of each area.'[17] A new QUANGO, the LGCE, was established to undertake the review and to make recommendations to the Secretary of State for the Environment. This was quite different from the situation in Scotland and Wales, where the respective Secretaries of State decided to undertake the structural reviews themselves. Also, unlike 1974, the country was not to be reviewed as a whole, but with the review taking place on a rolling area-by-area basis. There was to be no 'big bang' reorganisation. England was divided into five disparate groups of counties. The first 'tranche' comprised ten counties. Avon, Gloucestershire and Somerset were taken together, as were Humberside, Lincolnshire and North Yorkshire, and Cleveland with County Durham. The other two county areas in the first tranche were the Isle of Wight and Derbyshire, geographically isolated from the other areas being reviewed.

Government guidance to the LGCE on how to evaluate proposals for change indicated that as well as the financial costs and benefits a number of less tangible costs and benefits were seen as relevant:

Identity: How well do proposals reflect community identities and loyalties?

Accessibility: Will services be more or less accessible to individual communities if particular proposals are implemented?

Responsiveness: What opportunities exist for responsive local government reflecting community preferences under the different proposals put forward?

Democracy: To what extent will different proposals allow democratic units of local government, accountable to their constituent communities, to be introduced or maintained?[18]

The apparent willingness to consider retention of the two-tier system in some areas left open what proved to be a fatal chink in the armour (a chink which the new government has so far retained). Taken together with the aim of achieving 'the structure which best matches the particular circumstances of each area'[19] it virtually invited authorities to open up a campaign which best served their own future interests. A gladiatorial contest was thus set in place with, in broad terms, counties and districts on opposite sides of the arena.

The LGCE began its programme of work in the Isle of Wight in August 1992 and had produced draft recommendations for all first tranche areas by

June 1993,[20] compounding the problem of its flawed remit by failing to set out, and adhere to, a clear and common set of principles for restructuring. Commissioners took different views and different approaches and, as a result, the emerging proposals had the appearance of having more to do with their varying preferences than with any real variations in local circumstances. Table 1 shows the initial proposals from the LGCE; proposals which caused widespread disquiet and discontent. One northern council neatly summarised feelings by referring to the plans as 'Shambleshire'.[21]

TABLE 1
INITIAL PROPOSALS FOR THE FIRST TRANCHE AREAS

County Area	Existing No. of Local Authorities (County & Districts)	Proposals	
		New Unitary Authorities	Retained County & District Councils
Isle of Wight	3	1	Nil
Derbyshire	10	2	Nil
Cleveland	5	4	Nil
County Durham	9	2	Nil
Avon	7	4*	Nil
Gloucestershire	7	3	Nil
Somerset	6	1**	Nil
Lincolnshire	8	Nil	8
Humberside & North Yorkshire	19	7***	Nil

Notes:
* One authority includes territory transferred from the existing county of Somerset
** Part of the existing Mendip district is transferred to one of the new Avon authorities
*** One authority straddles the existing county boundary

These draft recommendations, containing as they did a mix of county-based unitaries, district-based unitaries, intermediate unitaries and *status quo*, without any discernible rhyme or reason, were thus generally seen to be arbitrary and unsustainable.

REVISED GUIDANCE

At government level, with the departure of Michael Heseltine from the Environment Department in early 1992 and his replacement by Michael Howard, the drive and enthusiasm behind the review seemed to be lost. The continuation of the review probably had more to do with the government wishing to avoid an embarrassing U-turn than a commitment to the process as such, but it was a policy no longer fully under control. In 1993 an attempt by John Gummer, who had become Secretary of State for the Environment in July, effectively to close down the review and move to a more selective approach was rejected by the Prime Minister. Thereafter the policy seems to have become one of simply trying to complete the process that had been set in train, gradually transmuting into a damage-limitation exercise.

On 30 September 1993 John Gummer announced a speeding up of the review process and issued the draft of new guidance to the LGCE. The review was now to be completed in all areas by the end of 1994, and the government strengthened the presumption in favour of unitary local authorities replacing the two-tier system. Proposals to make existing authorities unitary authorities would now demand 'special scrutiny' and 'very large unitary authorities' would need 'special justification'.[22] Greatly increased importance was also attached to the achievement of local consensus. Mr Gummer said that he wanted the new authorities to be 'big enough to do the job and small enough to know the people'.[23] The Chief Executive of the LGCE, Martin Easteal, apparently interpreted this as indicating an ideal size of between 150,000 and 250,000 population.[24]

However, the future direction of the review remained unclear. In the face of public opposition to its initial proposals, the LGCE decided to drop its unitary authority proposals for Derbyshire and County Durham, and instead to recommend continuation of the existing two-tier system for most parts of those counties. Furthermore, Sir John Banham, Chairman of the Commission, reiterated the LGCE's independence saying that, 'The Commission must be free to manage the process as we see fit. To have continuous instructions [from the government] which get cancelled – and artificial deadlines – is simply trying to manage the process by remote control. We are not going to have it'.[25] The proposals for Gloucestershire were also subsequently amended to retention of the two-tier system, whilst in Somerset the proposed county-based unitary authority was broken into three. In a battle of wills John Gummer referred the amended recommendations for Derbyshire, County Durham and Gloucestershire back to the LGCE for further consideration.

A growing number of local authorities began beating a path to the courts seeking judicial reviews. After all, for authorities perceiving themselves to be at the losing end of the process there was little more to be lost by taking such a course of action and potentially much to be gained. Crucially, on 28 January 1994, in an action brought by Derbyshire and Lancashire County Councils, a sentence in the November 1993 revised policy guidance to the LGCE, stating that the government expected continuation of the two-tier structure would be 'the exception' and that it expected to see 'a substantial increase in the number of unitary authorities in both urban and rural areas',[26] was judged to be 'outwith the Secretary of State's powers to give guidance' and therefore 'unlawful'. Mr Justice Jowitt indicated that he felt the effect of the sentence was to undermine the statutory review criteria contained in the Local Government Act and add a further criterion. The practical effect of this judgment, which proved to be a major turning point in the LGR, was to change the review emphasis back to whether reorganisation was desirable and away from a presumption in its favour.

By January 1995 the LGCE had produced 'final' recommendation for all 39 shire counties. At this point the balance of recommendations was:

- Eighteen counties in which no change to the existing two-tier structure was proposed.

- Eleven counties in which generally one or two new unitary authorities were proposed, but otherwise with no change to the existing two-tier structure

- Ten counties in which a fully unitary solution was recommended.[27]

A NEW TWIST

On 2 March 1995 the Secretary of State of the Environment, John Gummer, announced both the 'resignation' of LGCE Chairman Sir John Banham and a fresh review of 'selected districts' to get under way that summer. Association of County Councils Secretary Robin Wendt was later to confess that this 're-review' 'came as a complete surprise to the ACC. A small number of references back [to the LGCE] had been expected, but nothing on this scale. In effect the government was envisaging as many more unitaries (21) as it had rejected (18) from previous LGCE recommendations'.[28]

The Secretary of State initially identified 18 districts as candidates for further review, a figure which grew to 21. These districts were identified for one or more of five stated reasons. There was also, perhaps, a sixth unstated reason. Firstly there were districts not recommended by the LGCE for unitary status but which were 'among the largest' non-metropolitan districts in England. These included Warrington and Northampton. Second came a group of districts which had a previous status either as county boroughs or as counties, including Exeter, Gloucester and Huntingdonshire. Third were some authorities contiguous to, but not wishing to be part of, areas already proposed for unitary status, namely 'the Brushlings' (Broxtowe, Rushcliffe, Gedling). Fourth came a justification of 'dense population', used in relation to Halton. Fifth was what might be termed a 'what the heck' category, applied to the so-called Thames Gateway area: 'Five districts almost fully covered by the Thames Gateway area do not have unitary status at present. I have already said that I propose to refer three of these ... to the Commission. Clearly therefore there is a case for referring the other two ... as well.'[29] The sixth, unstated, reason was perhaps that unitary ambitions were helped if you had a Minister or Shadow Minister as your Member of Parliament to put in a good word on your behalf. Districts in this category could have included Huntingdonshire (John Major), Peterborough (Brian Mawhinney), Rushcliffe (Kenneth Clarke) and Blackburn (Jack Straw), but apparently not Suffolk Coastal (John Gummer)! New guidance was also to be issued to the LGCE, which was itself to be 'reconstituted'.

Not for the first time, there was a lack of clear argument as many other areas could be said to be in a similar position to those districts included in the re-review list. However, as a damage limitation exercise, it did enable the government to begin an effective close-down of the review process. Most of the glaring anomalies were thus removed.

Only in Berkshire did significant dispute rumble on. The county of Berkshire has been accorded the unique distinction of being singled out for complete dismemberment, aside from the 'new' counties of Avon, Cleveland and Humberside. This was a left-over from recommendations of the original (Banham-led) LGCE but now looks extremely out of place. Grigsby comments that:

> The saga of Berkshire's demise is more suited to a television mini series than the everyday run of politics in the home counties ... There was personal animosity, misunderstanding, political intrigue, rumours of a threat to deselect a prominent MP if he did not toe the line – plus a large dose of the old fashioned cock up factor.[30]

Berkshire's fate was not finally sealed until July 1996.

THE END OF THE CONSERVATIVE'S LGR

On 14 March 1996 John Gummer announced his decisions on the LGCE's recommendation for the 21 're-review' districts and concluded a process begun by the Conservatives some five years earlier. In total the review has created 46 new unitary local authorities in England (see Appendix 1). One came into being in 1995, 13 in 1996, a further 13 in 1997, and the remaining 19 will take over their responsibilities in 1998. Most of shire England retains the two-tier structure of county and district councils. A great deal of this outcome would be easily recognisable to anyone familiar with the pre-1974 structure of local government. Indeed, as we have commented elsewhere, 'the resulting local government map of England could have been produced with relative ease in a couple of hours on a wet Tuesday afternoon'.[31]

Overall, though, there can be few who are fully satisfied with the way that the review has been conducted and few who are fully satisfied with the outcome. The best that can be said of the outcome is that, as one of our research respondents put it, it has almost a logic. But it is a logic containing many anomalies. Of course the new structures will work. They have to. But that cannot disguise the fact that the new hybrid structure of English local government contains a number of in-built instabilities. One of the most significant is that the interrelationship between towns and their hinterlands seems to have been largely ignored – although the 'mark 2' LGCE rediscovered this concept in some cases. Many of the boundaries of the new unitaries do not reflect the 'real' or 'functional' town. The scene is therefore set for a return to the pre-1974 squabbles between county boroughs and their neighbours without adequate means for these disputes to be resolved.

The new hybrid structure of local government has, in addition, once again set in place a higher order status to which shire districts can aspire. Before 1974 many district authorities saw county borough status as the pinnacle of achievement and recognition, and there were constant attempts to achieve this higher status. During the parliamentary passage of the 1888 legislation which created county boroughs their number grew from ten to 61.[32] Even though the conditions for elevation changed over the years, many more county boroughs were created before the 1974 reorganisation of local government. Unless and until there is a further comprehensive reorganisation of local government there will undoubtedly have to be some criteria established which set out ground rules for creating further unitary areas.

Most of the attention in the review has been on the creation of new unitary authorities. However, a significant outcome that has received rather less comment is the 'downsizing' of 19 county councils, which lose one or more districts from their territory. For instance, Buckinghamshire has lost just one district (Milton Keynes) but that one district represented some 30 per cent of that county's population, so the effects can be quite dramatic. In a further case, downsizing will lead to the creation of a completely new shire county council: the eastern end of Hereford & Worcester re-emerges as Worcestershire.

A further 'hidden effect' of the review is the impact on one particular local government service – namely fire. Until now the fire service has been an integrated part of the local government structure, each service being a department of the respective county council. The reorganisations resulting from the review will lead to 24 of the 39 shire county fire services coming under the control of joint authorities. There are clear dangers in this structure and the finances of a number of the new bodies are already problematic.[33] Councillor Mick Warner, the last chair of the ACC's Fire and

Emergency Planning Committee, noted that 'A major task for new Combined Fire Authority members will be to ensure that the service remains clearly part of local government.'[34]

The LGR has been severely damaging. It has probably not produced a durable structure. It has brought out some of the worst in both national and local government. Although there have been some positives, the negatives surely predominate. There has been an enormous diversion of effort, away from local community and service concerns, and towards the LGR battle. The abiding memory of the review for all who have been involved with, or observed, its twists and turns must surely be that it has been an object lesson in how not to do things.

LESSONS FOR THE NEW GOVERNMENT

The key lesson for Labour in government is that it must be clear about its objectives for any new rounds of local government reorganisation, and state those objectives clearly and unambiguously. The temptation to play with maps seems irresistible but a better focus would be on responsibilities and processes. Reorganising structures provides no guarantee of better local government. That the new government intends to introduce the beginnings of regional government is clear. That this requires a single tier of unitary local government is less clear. It is to be hoped that the government can be persuaded to detach the issues from each other.

APPENDIX 1
THE NEW UNITARY AUTHORITIES IN SHIRE ENGLAND

From 1995	Isle of Wight
From 1996	Bath and North East Somerset
	Bristol
	East Riding of Yorkshire
	Hartlepool
	Kingston-upon-Hull
	Middlesbrough
	North East Lincolnshire
	North Lincolnshire
	North Somerset
	Redcar and Cleveland
	South Gloucestershire
	Stockton-on-Tees
	York
From 1997	Bournemouth
	Brighton and Hove
	Darlington
	Derby
	Leicester

Luton
Milton Keynes
Poole
Portsmouth
Rutland
Southampton
Stoke-on-Trent
Swindon

From 1998   Blackburn with Darwen
Blackpool
Bracknell Forest
Halton
Herefordshire
Medway Towns
Newbury
Nottingham
Peterborough
Plymouth
Reading
Slough
Southend-on-Sea
Thurrock
Torbay
Warrington
Windsor and Maidenhead
Wokingham
Wrekin

NOTES

1. *New Labour: Because Britain Deserves Better* (The Labour Party, 1997), p.33.
2. Ibid.
3. *A Choice for England* (The Labour Party, 1995), p.1.
4. *New Labour: Because Britain Deserves Better*, p.34.
5. Ibid., pp.34–5.
6. *A Choice for England*, p.19.
7. *New Labour: Because Britain Deserves Better*, p.34.
8. *A Choice for England*, p.20.
9. Ibid.
10. Ibid., p.19.
11. Ibid., p.20.
12. Ibid.
13. *Municipal Journal*, 31 May 1996, p.5.
14. Statement by the Secretary of State for the Environment (Michael Heseltine), 21 March 1991.
15. Ibid.
16. Department of the Environment, *Local Government Review: The Structure of Local Government in England: A Consultation Paper,* April 1991, para.3.
17. Ibid., para.27.
18. Department of the Environment, *Policy Guidance to the Local Government Commission for England,* July 1992, p.23.
19. Department of the Environment, *Local Government Review: The Structure of Local Government in England: A Consultation Paper,* para.27.
20. Local Government Commission for England reports: *The Future Local Government of the*

Isle of Wight (Dec. 1992), *of Cleveland and Durham* (May 1993), *of Derbyshire* (May 1993), *of Avon, Gloucestershire and Somerset* (June 1993), *The Future of Local Government for the Area North of the Humber* (June 1993), *The Future of Local Government from the Humber to the Wash* (June 1993).

21. *The Guardian*, 22 June 1993.
22. Department of the Environment, *Draft Revised Policy Guidance to the Local Government Commission for England*, Sept. 1993.
23. *The Birmingham Post*, 7 Oct. 1993.
24. *The Financial Times*, 20 Oct. 1993.
25. *The Financial Times*, 21 Oct. 1993.
26. Department of the Environment, *Policy Guidance to the Local Government Commission for England*, Nov. 1993.
27. Local Government Commission for England reports: *The Future Local Government of the Isle of Wight* (April 1993), *of Derbyshire* (Nov. 1993), *of Cleveland and County Durham* (Nov. 1993), *of Avon, Gloucestershire and Somerset* (Dec. 1993), *of Humberside, Lincolnshire and North Yorkshire* (Jan. 1994), *of Bedfordshire* (Oct. 1994), *of Buckinghamshire* (Oct. 1994), *of Cambridgeshire* (Oct. 1994), *of Cheshire* (Oct. 1994), *of Cumbria* (Oct. 1994), *of Hampshire* (Oct. 1994), *of Kent* (Oct. 1994), *of Lancashire* (Oct. 1994), *of Oxfordshire* (Oct. 1994), *of Berkshire* (Dec. 1994), *of County Durham (2nd review)* (Dec. 1994), *of Devon* (Dec. 1994), *of Dorset* (Dec. 1994), *of East Sussex* (Dec. 1994), *of Essex* (Dec. 1994), *of Hereford and Worcester* (Dec. 1994), *of Leicestershire* (Dec. 1994), *of Norfolk* (Dec. 1994), *of Northamptonshire* (Dec. 1994), *of Northumberland* (Dec. 1994), *of Nottinghamshire* (Dec. 1994), *of Staffordshire* (Dec. 1994), *of Suffolk* (Dec. 1994), *of Surrey* (Dec. 1994), *of Warwickshire* (Dec. 1994), *of West Sussex* (Dec. 1994), *of Wiltshire* (Dec. 1994), *of Cornwall* (Jan. 1995), *of Derbyshire (2nd review)* (Jan. 1995), *of Gloucestershire (2nd review)* (Jan. 1995), *of Hertfordshire* (Jan. 1995), *of Shropshire* (Jan. 1995).
28. Robin Wendt, *The Last Word?* (Association of County Councils, 1997), p.11.
29. John Gummer, 2 March 1995.
30. John Grigsby, 'Bringing Down the Curtain on the Royal County of Berkshire', *County News*, Vol.89, No.6 (Oct. 1996), p.16.
31. Howard Davis, *England Under Review* (The British Library, 1997), p.1.
32. Bryan Keith-Lucas and Peter G. Richards, *A History of Local Government in the Twentieth Century* (George Allen and Unwin, 1978), p.13.
33. Howard Davis, 'Politically Weak and Financially Vulnerable: Britain's New Fire Authorities', *Fire Cover*, No.135 (Spring 1997), pp.52–3
34. Association of County Councils, *Combining for Success* (1995), p.3.

The Local Government Review: A 'Policy Process' Perspective

INTRODUCTION

The Local Government Review which was undertaken between 1991 and 1996 in England and (on a different basis) in Scotland and Wales has already proved a rich source of academic insights and analysis. An expanding body of literature, to which this author has contributed, has examined various aspects of this perplexing and controversial policy initiative.[1] The main focus of analysis so far has been the politics of the process, and has involved in particular attempts to make sense of the changing objectives and public stances of the key actors – institutional and individual – and the strategies and tactics deployed to maximise the probability of preferred outcomes. This has been the main theme of a number of case studies focusing on events in particular counties, and also of a number of attempts to provide 'overview' interpretations.[2]

This political focus is understandable, because the Local Government Review (LGR) process raised a number of fascinating political questions – What did the government really want or expect from the English review? Why, if they were committed to unitary authorities, did they so readily accept the predominantly no-change proposals of the Local Government Commission (LGC)? Why did so many district councils support proposals which implied their own disappearance? All these questions have provided formidable challenges for political analysts.[3]

However, there is a different aspect of the LGR which merits further academic attention. The review, in England at least, started out as a serious piece of policy analysis in an extremely complex field of study. The very fact that Commission was appointed to make recommendations signalled the expectation that a rigorous analytical approach would be adopted. As Michael Clarke has pointed out:

> We have a distinguished history of Committees and Commissions of enquiry in this country. What distinguishes them is that they collect

---

Steve Leach, De Montfort University.

evidence, sift and weight what they discover, expose the possibilities through logic and rational argument and make a carefully-crafted set of recommendations. I fear that the Commission denies all of this.[4]

Indeed, the appointment of a Commission has traditionally been the main way in which British governments have tackled problems of local government reorganisation. In this sense the abolition of the GLC and the metropolitan counties in the 1983–86 period, and the way in which local government has been reorganised recently in Scotland and Wales, can be regarded as aberrations. The complexity of redesigning a local government system and in particular the challenge of balancing and synthesising a whole range of often disparate considerations has typically and, arguably, rightly caused governments to be wary of DIY solutions. The appointment of the Banham Commission in 1992 confirmed, in England at least, that this tradition of 'arms-length analysis' had been restored.

Some preliminary analysis of the applicability of different policy process models to the LGR process has already been undertaken.[5] However, this analysis was carried out at a relatively early stage in the LGC's programme of work, and several changes of emphasis on and interpretation of different criteria subsequently occurred. With the government's acceptance of the final recommendations of the second Commission (chaired by Sir David Cooksey) the whole strange process can now be reviewed retrospectively in its entirety.

Whilst recognising the rationalist expectations implicit in the setting up of any form of Commission, the work of what was in effect a 'departmental Commission', studying a politically controversial topic is never likely to enjoy an existence unaffected by political pressures and considerations. In a Royal Commission, policy analysis and political influence are rigorously separated out, with the latter involved in setting the terms of reference at the beginning and responding to the recommendations at the end, but by tradition playing no part *during* the Commission's deliberative process. A departmental Commission is more vulnerable to political influence during the course of its deliberations.[6] It has to cope with an interplay of political influence and the expectation of rational analysis.

Although the final *outcome* of the LGR in England has been undeniably incremented (see Table 3) it is not plausible to argue that the process which led to this outcome was incremented in nature. As Table 3 shows, at one stage the LGC's recommendations pointed to a radical restructuring of local government, including the disappearance of county councils (and the two-tier system) in over half of the current English counties. Of more relevance are the 'rational' and 'garbage can' models of policy process. During the LGR process it often appeared as though the two models were in competition as explanatory mechanisms!

The rational model, a familiar tool of analysis and prescription, whose influence has survived many attempts to marginalise it, may be characterised as follows:[7]

(i)   there is a clear unambiguous statement of what problem is being addressed (and/or what key objective is being sought);

(ii)   there is a list of the criteria (preferably in priority order), on the basis of which the potential effectiveness of different solutions can be assessed;

(iii) information about the present and future characteristics of the relevant policy variables is systematically collected and analysed;

(iv)   there is a wide and unencumbered search for solutions, from which a 'short-list' of possible options can be drawn up;

(v)   the options are systematically evaluated on the basis of the criteria set out at stage (ii) and the information collected at stage (iii).

The garbage can model, first conceptualised by Cohen, March and Olsen, has the following characteristics.[8]

(i)   Goal or preference setting is not as neat and clear-cut as suggested by the rational model. Goals may be ill-defined, contradictory, confused or fuzzy. The garbage can model further suggests that preferences may be defined by action rather than precede it. Decision makers may discover their preferences through action.

(ii)   A second core characteristic of the garbage can model is unclear technology. In short, policy makers operate under the disadvantage that they lack a clear misunderstanding of how to achieve their goals. The world is complex and how to intervene in it effectively may be beyond the grasp of decision makers.

(iii) A third feature is fluid participation. Policy makers drift in and out of the debate. Sometimes the attention of key policy makers is drawn to other issues and a new set of decision makers moves into the frame.

(iv)   Problems and goals are not defined, so that solutions can be sought through a careful review of the evidence. The Garbage Can Model suggests that it is more realistic to see policy making as determined by four streams: problems, solutions, participants and choice opportunities. Each of the streams has its own life and relates to its partners in a fairly random way. Policy making is 'a collection of choices looking for problems, issues and feelings looking for decision situations in which they might be aired, solutions looking for issues to which they might be the answer, and decision makers looking for work'.

Although a veneer of rational analysis was sustained throughout the review process, the application of its principles was severely flawed.[9] Superficially, the garbage can model appears more congruent with the operation of the process. But to characterise the LGR process predominantly in 'garbage can' terms is perhaps unfair and does not do justice to the rational intentions (and to a lesser extent achievements) of the LGC. In retrospect, the process is perhaps best characterised as a fluid one, in which problems and solutions became *intertwined*. Tentative solutions were proferred and then reassessed in the light of new evidence about their impact, or in the light of a reassessment of the nature of the problem. In principle, this process sounds like an impressive example of a learning system in action. Instead of attempting to identify a high-risk 'single solution', the LGC allowed the best solution to emerge organically, following an extended period of experimentation. In reality it was not quite like that, but the idea of a continuous interplay between perceptions of the problem and perceptions of the solution does capture an important facet of the LGC's mode of operation.

The remainder of this article is structured as follows. The criteria of choice addressed by the LGC at various times in their operations are identified and classified, and some 'missing criteria' also highlighted. Then the different 'solutions' available to and recommended by the LGC at various stages are identified. The main section of the article follows through the interplay of problems and solutions in an analysis of the changing pattern of recommendations over the life of the Banham Commission (and its successor). Finally some conclusions about the key characteristics of the policy process involved are drawn.

THE CRITERIA OF EVALUATION

As the summary of the main characteristics of the rational model indicates (see page 20 above), one of its key requirements is an explicit listing of the criteria that will be used to assess the solutions. The 1992 Local Government Act required the LGC to determine what type of structure would better 'reflect the identities and interests of local communities' and 'secure effective and convenient local government'. The implication that the current two-tier system was not necessarily the best vehicle for meeting these requirements is the nearest thing we have to an official statement of the problem. The LGC soon added a third key criterion: 'ensuring that the change is worthwhile and cost-effective over time'.

The Policy Guidance provided a further set of more detailed criteria to the point of confusion, some of them relating to accountability issues (for example, a concern with the accountability implications of joint arrangements), others relating to particular services (with a strong concern about the survival of a viable strategic planning function) and a whole host of criteria concerning various aspects of accessibility, identity, responsiveness and democracy welded unhelpfully together into something called a community index. Joint arrangements and the failure of the structure planning system were subsequently taken seriously by the Commission; the community index was wisely ignored.

In an earlier paper by the author an attempt was made to instil some logic into this pot-pourri of criteria. In it, three different functions of local governement were identified:[10]

- local government as a political mechanism for diffusing power;

- local government as a vehicle for the expression of values of community;

- local government as a mechanism for allocating goods and services, which cannot be provided through the market.

The third of these functions reflects the role of local government as a service provider (or enabler). The second recognises the centrality of 'community' as a basis for local government. The first raises issues about the role of local government above and beyond that of a provider (or enabler) of services, and also questions about forms of accountability.

The service provision role was expressed in the LGC's work in its concern for the costs of various solutions and also for their impact on some (although by no means all) services. 'Community' was a major concern throughout. What the Commission never really got to grips with was the role of local government, and in particular to what extent a wider (as opposed to a narrower) enabling role is regarding as a legitimate consideration. Consideration of accountability – beyond a concern with joint arrangements – were also never convincingly incorporated.

Four primary criteria of evaluation and ten secondary criteria – reflecting the above roles – can be identified as 'worthy of consideration' in a local government review (see Table 1). As we shall see, some of these were taken seriously by the LGC throughout, some moved off and on to the agenda during the period the Commission operated and others were largely ignored.

TABLE 1

THE CRITERIA OF EVALUATION IN THE LOCAL GOVERNMENT REVIEW

A   **Cost-Effectiveness of Service Provision**
        The capacity to provide cost-effective local services which meet local needs.

        This criteria can be sub-divided into two components.

A(1)   *Costs and savings*, a criteria which incorporates both the *'operational costs'* of running
        services in the proposed new system compared with the existing system and the costs of
        moving from one system to another (that is, the *transitional costs* of reorganisation).

A(2)   The *effectiveness* or *quality* of service provision in the proposed new system compared
        with the existing system as assessed by such measure as accessibility, responsiveness to
        local needs, reliability and level of inter-service co-ordination (for those services which
        require it).

B   **Community Responsiveness**
        The capacity to express and respond to the pattern of community identity and behaviour
        in the area.

        This criteria can be divided into three components.

B(1)   *Perceived identity:* the communities, including but not limited to the spatial area(s) to
        which people feel that they belong, or with which they identify.

B(2)   *Patterns of activity:* what people actually do, as opposed to what they say, their patterns
        of behaviour in relation to work, education, shopping and leisure.

B(3)   *Expressed preferences:* what people say they would prefer (in relation to local
        government structure) in an exercise which sets out options.

C   **Democratic Viability**
        The capacity to incorporate and express principles of healthy local democracy.

C(1)   *Clarity of accountability; political* and *financial* accountability can be differentiated
        here.

C(2)   *Public comprehensibility:* the level of understanding shown by the public about the
        allocation of responsibilities within the system.

C(3)   *Political and public participation:* the extent to which the system encourages active
        participation by *local councillors* (councillor numbers and councillor roles) and by *local
        people* (through mechanisms of participative democracy).

D   **Governmental Capacity**
        The capacity to carry out the wider tasks of local government effectively.

D(1)   *Strategic capacity:* the capacity to plan future investment in and around the local areas
        and to develop a strategic view of the future of the local area within a regional or sub-
        regional context.

D(2)   *Networking capacity:* the extent to which an authority can achieve its strategic priorities
        and 'get things done' by influencing and working with other agencies (public, private
        and voluntary).

THE TYPES OF SOLUTIONS

There were in principle five different forms of solution available to the Commission, three of them unitary in nature, one involving no change (that is, retaining the *status quo*) and one involving a hybrid (that is, a mixture of unitary and *status quo*). Ironically, in the first tranche of recommendations, it was assumed by the Commission that it was not possible to recommend hybrid solutions in any one county. By the end of the process, hybrid solutions were one of the most prevalent forms of recommendation.

Unitary Solutions

(1) *Unitary County*

   A solution in which the whole of a county becomes a single unitary authority – this definition has been extended to include counties recommended for county-wide unitary status with the exception of a single district (recommended for separate unitary status).

(2) *Unitary District*

   A solution in which all the existing districts in a county are recommended for unitary status.

(3) *Unitary Intermediate*

   A solution in which counties are sub-divided (or districts amalgamated) into a set of unitary authorities.

(4) *No Change*

   A solution in which the *status quo* is retained for the whole county area.

(5) *Hybrid*

   A solution in which the *status quo* is retained for the whole county area, with the exception of one or two recommended unitary authorities within it.

THE CHANGING RELATIONSHIPS BETWEEN PROBLEMS AND SOLUTIONS

For the purposes of analysis, it is possible to divide the output of the LGC into four distinct stages. The first stage covers the period up to May 1993, by which time the LGC had produced draft recommendations for all the ten county areas of the first tranche. The second stage covers the period between summer 1993 and summer 1994, when the LGC produced its draft recommendations for the remaining 29 county areas, and its final recommendations for the first ten county areas (three of which were subsequently 'referred back'). The third stage covers the period up to July

1995, by which time the final recommendations had been published for the 29 counties not in the first tranche (and the three 'referred back' cases were also dealt with). The fourth stage, March 1995 to early 1996, covers the 21 specific cases for unitary status looked at by the Cooksey Commission (although there is a little temporal overlap between stages 1 and 2 and stages 2 and 3, they are separate enough to provide a useful analytical tool).

Table 2 sets out the recommendations made by the LGC at each of stages 1, 2 and 3 (stage 4 is dealt with separately), summarising the pattern of recommendations using the five categories of solution identified earlier. Table 4 identifies the main criteria that were used at each stage to justify the recommendations made. What we see clearly from Tables 2 and 3 is the inexorable movement from an emphasis on unitary recommendations to an emphasis on *status quo* and hybrid recommendations.

- In stage 1, there was only one example of a *status quo* recommendation with 90 per cent of the recommendations being for unitary solutions of one kind or another

- By stage 2, the balance had changed to 62 per cent unitary/38 per cent *status quo* (including hybrids)

- By stage 3, the balance had changed again to 12 per cent unitary/88 per cent *status quo* (including hybrids)

Looking within these broad categories, it is of note that solutions based on *unitary counties* (including those with one unitary district taken out) were an important feature of the stage 1 recommendations, but then disappeared from the solutions agenda (with the exception of Shropshire/Telford at stage 2). Recommendations for unitary district solutions were never a serious contender (the only exceptions being Cleveland and Berks). 'Intermediate unitary' solutions featured prominently at stage 1 (40 per cent) were the single most popular solution at stage 2 (55 per cent) but dropped spectacularly by stage 3 (12 per cent). *Status quo* proposals were negligible at stage 1, slightly more prevalent by stage 2, but dominated stage 3 (52 per cent). Hybrids were not considered at stage 1 (the Commission's perception of the time was that it could not recommend a hybrid solution within its terms of reference, but emerged strongly at stage 2 (25 per cent), an emergence that was sustained at stage 3 (36 per cent). The final local government map which emerged as a result of the review process and intermediate unitary solutions contain more hybrid and fewer *status quo* solutions because of recommendations of the Cooksey Committee, which affected five counties previously earmarked for no change, and because of the government's rejection of five 'intermediate unitary' solutions.[11]

In summary, it was clear at stage 1 the LGC had a strong preference for unitary solutions, predominantly CC-based or amalgamations of districts. At stage 2, its dominant preferences were for unitary amalgamations and hybrid solutions. By stage 3, it had shifted its view to a preference for *status quo* and hybrid solutions. What lies behind these changes in view? In so far as a rational process can be identified the changes can best be understood in terms of the *weighting* given to the different criteria identified on page 23 above.

TABLE 2

THE COMMISSION'S PROPOSALS IN DETAIL

	Phase 1 Draft Recommendations	Phase 2 Final Recommendations and Draft Recommendations	Phase 3 Final Recommendations
1. AVON	DC AMALG	DC AMALG	
2. BEDS		DC AMALG	DC AMALG
3. BERKS		DC AMALG	UNITARY DC
4. BUCKS		DC AMALG	DC AMALG
5. CAMBS		DC AMALG	S/Q
6. CHES		DC AMALG	S/Q
7. CLEVELAND	UNITARY DC	UNITARY DC	
8. CORNWALL		S/Q	S/Q
9. CUMBRIA		DC AMALG	S/Q
10. DERBYSHIRE	UNITARY CC	HYBRID	HYBRID
11. DEVON		HYBRID	HYBRID
12. DORSET		DC AMALG	DC AMALG
13. DURHAM	UNITARY CC	HYBRID	HYBRID
14. EAST SUSSEX		DC AMALG	HYBRID
15. ESSEX		HYBRID	HYBRID
16. GLOUCS	DC AMALG	S/Q	S/Q
17. HANTS		HYBRID	HYBRID
18. HEREFORD & WORCS		DC AMALG	HYBRID
19. HERTS		S/Q	S/Q
20. HUMBERSIDE	DC AMALG	DC AMALG	
21. ISLE OF WIGHT	UNITARY CC	UNITARY CC	
22. KENT		HYBRID	S/Q
23. LANCS		DC AMALG	S/Q
24. LEICS		HYBRID	HYBRID
25. LINCS	S/Q	S/Q	
26. NORFOLK		DC AMALG	
27. NORTHUMBERLAND		S/Q	S/Q
28. NORTHANTS		DC AMALG	S/Q
29. NORTH YORKSHIRE	DC AMALG	DC AMALG	
30. NOTTS		HYBRID	HYBRID
31. OXON		DC AMALG	S/Q
32. SHROPS		UNITARY CC	HYBRID
33. SOMERSET	UNITARY CC	DC AMALG	
34. STAFFS		HYBRID	HYBRID
35. SUFFOLK		DC AMALG	S/Q
36. SURREY		DCAMALG	S/Q
37. WARKS		DC AMALG	S/Q
38. WEST SUSSEX		HYBRID	S/Q
39. WILTS		DC AMALG	HYBRID
TOTAL	**10**	**39**	**32**

TABLE 3
THE COMMISSION'S PROPOSAL: A SUMMARY

	Phase 1		Phase 2		Phase 3	
	No	%	No	%	No	%
Unitary Solutions						
Unitary County	4	40	2	5	0	
Unitary Districts	1	10	1	2	1	3
DC Amalgamations	4	40	21	55	3	9
Total Unitary	**9**	**90**	**24**	**623**	**4**	**12**
Status Quo Solutions						
Status Quo	1	10	5	12	16	52
Hybrid	0		10	25	12	36
Total Status Quo	**1**	**10**	**15**	**38**	**8**	**88**
No. of Authorities	**(10)**		**(39)**		**(32)**	

THE INTERPLAY OF PROBLEMS AND SOLUTIONS

The strange interplay between problems (or criteria of choice) and solutions was exemplified at a relatively early stage in the LGC's operations. Derbyshire was one of the first counties to which the Commissioners were despatched (in pairs). On the Chairman's first visit, he reportedly advised the assembled local authority representatives that there was no point in arguing *either* for a unitary county solution *or* a solution based on unitary districts:[12] a strange pre-emption indeed of a pair of logically viable solutions, before a shred of evidence had been collected. This was not an auspicious start.

STAGE 1: THE FIRST TEN DRAFT RECOMMENDATIONS

By the time the first set of draft recommendations appeared, the LGC appeared to have changed its mind about the viability of these two forms of solutions. A unitary county solution was proposed in Somerset and the Isle of Wight and (if the definition is stretched slightly) in Derbyshire (with Derby a separate authority) and Durham (Darlington likewise). A unitary district-based solution was proposed for Cleveland (see Table 2). In reaching its first set of recommendations, in which it has to be acknowledged the threads of consistency were not always clear. The LGC relied heavily on the criteria of costs and savings in service provision (as assessed in the financial model provided by Ernst and Young), and community identity (as assessed in the MORI survey). There was a selective attempt to include considerations of service effectiveness, and a limited attempt to incorporate considerations of political accountability (primarily in terms of the need for joint arrangements) networking capacity and public comprehensibility. These points are illustrated below.

COSTS AND SAVINGS

The Ernst and Young model where findings were accepted without reservation by the LGC (despite a significant amount of countervailing evidence[13]) implied an overall increase in costs for solutions involving relatively small unitary authorities (around half the current number of districts, or more) and a steadily increasing level of savings as the number of unitaries decreased, with maximum savings implied for a single unitary authority (up to a population of one million). This financial assessment played a large part in the LGC's early propensity to recommend large unitary authorities. In Derbyshire, for example, 'A single unitary authority, serving 700,000 *would* save around £16 million per year for the county as a whole, a larger saving than could be obtained for any option other than a unitary authority for the whole of Derbyshire'.[14] Similar arguments were set out in support of the other three county-based solutions (and for the large proposed new unitaries in the North and East Ridings of Yorkshire).

COMMUNITY IDENTITY

One of the challenges for the Commission was that the evidence based on the MORI survey of community identity – itself open to a good deal of criticism[15] – did not always point in the same direction as the evidence on costs and savings. Where it did there was no problem of conflicting criteria for the LGC to resolve. In the Durham report, for example, it was argued that 'County Durham has a stronger identity than any other county in the first tranche and a stronger identity than the districts in County Durham'.[16] In Humberside, Avon, Cleveland, Gloucestershire and North Yorkshire, however, where the community identity evidence either favoured the districts or was inconclusive, a 'sub-county' solutions was recommended. Maximisation of savings was traded for strength of community identity.

Although at this stage the main area of debate was between 'costs and savings' and 'community identity', other criteria did receive some attention, often as subsidiary justification for a recommendation reached on other premises. For example, *service effectiveness* for *certain* services was discussed, and perceived to strengthen the case for larger unitary authorities.[17] Many crucial service areas, however, including education social service and housing, were largely ignored in this part of the debate. *Networking capacity* was also cited in support of larger (preferably county-based) unitaries.[18] The concern with *political accountability,* assessed in terms of the loss of accountability that would follow from the need for joint arrangements, was also discussed and pointed in same direction.[19] And *public comprehensibility* was used to underline the case for unitary solutions *per se* as opposed to the retention of the *status quo.*[20]

Indeed, several of these criteria were spelled out in a section which appeared in all of the first set of reports entitled 'The Case for Unitary Authorities'. However, in none of the reports (with one exception) was there a parallel section drawing attention to the case for the two-tier system. Bizarrely, such a section *was* included in the final reports of the first series, which covered Humberside/Lincolnshire south of the Humber,[21] a further example of a proneness to inconsistency within the LGC at this stage.

In summary, an analysis of the attempts by the LGC to interrelate problems and solutions at Stage One reveals the following features:

(i)   A predisposition towards unitary solutions involving relatively large authorities (in terms of population and territory).

(ii) An emphasis on the criteria of costs and savings and community identity, as assessed in the two commissioned pieces of consultancy.

(iii) A significantly stronger community identity on the part of districts (or some districts) *vis-à-vis* the county was used to justify a sub-county unitary recommendation (typically singling out districts with a particularly high level of community identity for unitary status on existing boundaries – for example, Forest of Dean).

(iv) A lower priority concern with public comprehensibility (which favoured unitary solutions), political accountability (which favoured county scale unitaries, because of the lack of joint arrangements needed), service effectiveness (on a selective basis) and networking capacity. Both the latter were judged as favouring larger unitaries.

There was also some indication in the 'South of the Humber Report', that the existing ability of authorities to work together was a significant consideration, though 'existing performance' criteria had been expressly *excluded* elsewhere.[22]

Criteria that were absent, or only marginally involved, were *service effectiveness* in relation to a whole range of 'personal' services (education, social services, housing), *governmental capacity,* an omission which reflected the lack of any serious discussion of the role of local authorities (beyond some glib and insubstantial reference to 'enabling'[23]) and *patterns of activity.* This last criteria, which played such a big part in the Redcliffe-Maud Commission's considerations, was alluded to from time to time,[24] but invariably discounted because of the *preferences* of those who would be affected (for example, by an extension of an existing city-based district's boundaries). Although the future weight the LGC would place on *expressed preference* – that is, public opinion – was not highlighted in these Stage 1 reports, the signs were there, particularly in relation to the response to the above-mentioned city boundary extension dilemma.

There were several flaws in the analysis carried out by the LGC at Stage 1 – for instance, the lack of a serious response to the most striking feature of the MORI Community Identity issues, namely that by far the strongest level of identification of local people was with neighbourhood village and town rather than county *or* district, both of which lagged well behind. However, at this stage it could be argued that the LGC was still making a serious attempt to develop recommendations from an analysis of evidence relating to pre-stated criteria. A preference for unitary solutions had developed not because the government appeared to favour them (that was less apparent then) but because the LGC's reading of evidence pointed in that direction, except in certain types of county area (the rural fringe). The rational model was still viable as an explanatory device, whatever the *limitations* in its application by the LGC.

STAGE 2 : THE RESPONSE TO THE CHANGE IN GUIDANCE

By the time of Stage 2, this veneer of the rationality had all but disappeared. In October 1993, the government had announced some fundamental changes concerning the conduct of the review. First it was to be speeded up, with a programme that required final recommendations for all county areas by the end of 1994. Secondly, the expectation that the Commission would recommend unitary solutions was greatly strengthened with a new clause which stated: 'but the Government expects this [the continuation of the two-tier structure] to be the exception, and the result will be a substantial increase in the number of unitary authorities in both urban and rural areas'.[25] Other elements in the guidance steered the LGC away from recommending unitary authorities with a very large area (for community identity reasons), and away from unitary authorities with relatively small populations (for service effectiveness reasons).[26] In an accompanying press statement, it became clear that the Commission was expected to attract particular weight to *intermediate unitary solution* – sub-division of counties or amalgamation of districts.[27]

In accepting – or appearing to accept – this switch in its terms of reference, which amounted to a change from a brief that emphasised *input* criteria and did not restrict the search for viable solutions to a brief which emphasised *output* criteria, and explicitly precluded or limited the scope for recommending solutions other than intermediate unitary solution, it can be argued that the LGC ceded its right to be taken seriously as a Commission, within the normal expectations of the behaviour of such bodies. Faced with a demand to discard rational analysis (clarify the criteria of choice, analyse the evidence, reach a conclusion) and to accept a requirement to produce a specific solution, it can be argued that the only course open to an honourable Commission was resignation. This did not happen. The LGC accepted its new terms of reference, whilst the chair made some bizarre statements about 'the need to sell unitary authorities to the public'[28] (a strange interpretation indeed of a Commission's role), and agreed to reconsider final recommendations for two-tier (or hybrid) solutions made in relation to Derbyshire, Durham and Gloucestershire (though not, strangely, in Lincolnshire).

The LGC now had a difficult balancing act. They had accepted the requirement to recommend a specific solution. But they had to continue to operate in the normal way of a Commission, and in particular to produce coherent reports reflecting superficially at least the requirements of the rational model. They were also still operating within policy guidance which contained all the previous criteria concerning costs, service effectiveness, accountability, and so on. Their task appeared now to ensure that the evidence somehow fitted the required recommendation. Garbage can explanations of the policy process began to look much more credible.

The Commission, in their search for a way out, indicated that the ability of the authorities in a county to agree on an intermediate unitary solution would be an important influence on the Commission's recommendations[29] (it was not clear whether this agreement was supposed to include the county council, or merely all the districts involved).

The publication of the LGC's final recommendation for the ten county areas in tranche 1 straddled the government's announcement on 1 October 1994 of the change in the rules. Those which preceded it had already indicated some switch in the LGC's handling of the relationship between problems and solutions.

- *public preference* – as expressed through the second MORI survey – was now being given considerable weight, although this had not been signalled at Stage 1;
- *costs and savings* began to be reinterpreted as a criterion which excluded certain types of solution (for example, small unitaries) but where the requirement was now that the proposed solution financially should break-even (rather than maximise the savings potential of large size);
- *status quo solutions* also increased in prominence, mainly as a reflection of the emphasis on public preference. In several counties, local residents had been unconvinced by arguments for a unitary solution.

Thus the final recommendation of the Tranche One areas included four *status quo* or hybrid recommendations[30] and six unitary recommendations, one county-based (Isle of Wight), one district-based (Cleveland) and four consisting of intermediate unitary solutions. The recommendations for Somerset involved a particularly unconvincing *volte-face*. More emphasis was placed on Somerset residents' preferences (on balance) for a unitary solution in principle, than on their lack of enthusiasm for any of the unitary alternatives suggested by the Commission! The government's intervention and the LGC's response confirmed the LGC's emergent view on how the 'costs and savings' criterion should be interpreted, but raised big questions about the extent to which the Commission could sustain both its new-found predisposition towards the *status quo* or its emphasis on public opinion, given the propensity of the public to opt for no change. Two new criteria/solutions emerged: intermediate unitary authorities as the preferred (or arguably required) solution and the ability of the authorities (or districts?) in a county area to reach consensus on such a solution.[31] This was the confused world of apparent changes in expectations, and rules, which faced the authorities who had to decide, late in 1994, what kind of submission to make to the LGC.

The draft recommendations for the 29 counties not so far considered, when they emerged, provided a strange mixture of *status quo* and intermediate unitary recommendation. Sometimes it seemed almost arbitrary whether the preferred recommendation was intermediate unitary (rather than *status quo*) or vice versa. What was apparent – in so far as any clear patterns could be identified – were the following priorities in relation to problems/solutions.

- *public preference* was signalled strongly as the likely decisive factor in the final recommendation, when it became known;
- *'costs and savings'* considerations were used as indicated earlier to set the limits of the search for unitary solutions – they were used to preclude district-based solutions and the search on 'intermediate unitary' solutions of around 150,000–200,000 in population size;
- *'intermediate unitary'* solutions were the most prevalent, this being the recommendation in over 60 per cent of the reports;
- *'status quo'* or *'hybrid'* solutions were still in the frame as far as the LGC were concerned, this being the recommendation in nearly 40 per cent of the reports.

Other criteria fell very much into the background, or were used selectively. Strength of community identity, for example, was used to justify the inclusion of a limited number of 'unitary authorities' in an otherwise *status quo* recommendation (for example, Rutland, Herefordshire, New Forest and

Thurrock). Joint arrangements were still being mentioned as an important consideration, but then often ignored in the recommendations which ensued. Service effectiveness had almost disappeared in a criteria, as had patterns of life and work and networking capacity. It was increasingly apparent that the choice of being narrowed down to *intermediate unitary* or *status quo* with public preference the likely ultimate arbiter.

The impoverished state the Commission's analytical process had now reached can be illustrated by the way in which the final recommendation is set out in almost any of the Stage 2 reports. The Cheshire report is typical. The Commission identify three 'possibilities for the structure of local government in Cheshire' (two intermediate unitary and one *status quo* minus Warrington) and concludes:

> Each of these structures has advantages and disadvantages. The arguments are finely balanced but ... the Commission has concluded that five unitary authorities based in revised district boundaries would provide the best structural arrangement for local government in Cheshire.[32]

That was it. No.summary of advantages and disadvantages with the weighting the LGC attached to them in reaching their decision was set out. Nor would it have been easy to deduce such a list from the previous contents of the report. Judged by the (admittedly demanding) criteria of the rational model, the Stage 1 report did at least go some way to meeting the requirements. The Stage 2 reports hardly bothered making the attempt.

STAGE 3: THE FINAL RECOMMENDATIONS

Although no one was clear about the extent of its influence at the time, the political context in which the Review was operated had been affected by the judgment issued in the judicial review, initiated by Lancashire and Derbyshire to question the legality of the new emphasis on unitary authorities in the revised Policy Guidance of October 1993. The High Court decided in January 1994 that the explicit inclusion of a government preference for unitary authorities was incompatible with the provisions of the 1992 Local Government Act, and ordered the deletion of the offending sentence quoted on page 30 above. The government did not take this judgment to appeal, although it continued to reaffirm its commitment to (intermediate) unitary solutions.

The Commission would, of course, have been aware of this judgment during the period in which they draw up their draft recommendations for the remaining 29 counties. There is evidence that it changed the climate of debate.[33] When the final recommendations were announced, it was clear that *status quo* or hybrid solutions were now dominant (see Table 3). The final reports, which were hardly more convincing as serious pieces of analysis than their predecessors, relied heavily on a single criteria – *public preference*. If the public's views – as measured by the LGC's own survey or (more importantly) through the MORI survey – favoured the *status quo*, the the *status quo* was recommended. If this was the case with the exception of one (or at most two) districts within which there was a clear preference for unitary status, then the Commission recommended a hybrid solution. In situations where the evidence did not point strongly in either direction, it sometimes recommended intermediate unitary solutions. In one case – to continue its record of inconsistency – it recommended an all-unitary district solution (Berkshire). In the event some of the Commission's few 'intermediate unitary' recommendations were rejected by the government, who substituted hybrid solutions (Bucks, Beds, Dorset, North Yorks). But that is another story, which has been documented elsewhere.[34]

Thus, by the end of the process little reference was being made to the other criteria which had been emphasised at earlier stages. Costs and savings had become reinterpreted as 'the solutions should not cost more in the medium term (5–10 years) taking into account transitional costs'. Both *status quo*, hybrids and intermediate unitary were perceived as meeting that criterion. Community identity had been almost wholly subsumed by public preference. Service effectiveness was never seriously analysed, although both hybrid and intermediate unitary solutions raised serious questions about the effectiveness of a range of services. Governmental capacity was never considered, networking capacity quickly neglected, accountability issues side-stepped. What started out as a reasonably wide-ranging review of the impact of different structures on a range of relevant criteria ended up as a public preference exercise in a situation where the public actually knew and cared little about the review.[35]

THE COOKSEY COMMISSION

There was a further twist to the review process when the government appointed a new commission to reconsider the case for unitary status for 21 districts considered (by the government) to be 'anomalies' in relation to the final pattern of recommendations. The interesting aspect of the Cooksey Commission's recommendation from the perspective of this paper is their unilateral introduction of a new criteria of evaluation – 'centrality':[36]

> where review districts are peripheral to their county settings in geographic, social economic or cultural terms, they may have a strong case for unitary status. Where the review district is central

> to the county setting, closely integrated with the life of the surrounding area, the case for the two-tier arrangement renaming in place will have more strength.

This was arguably the single most important criteria used by the Cocksey Commission. It is, of course, an interpretation of the 'pattern of life and work' criteria so comprehensively neglected by the Banham Commission. The new Commission continued to take into account public preference, but analysis shows that it was a less dominant concern for them.[37] The interesting implication is, of course, that the application of the concept of centrality *retrospectively* raises an issue of incompatibility. If centrality is important in Norfolk, Northampton and Gloucestershire, is it not equally so in Staffs, Leicestershire and Notts?

CONCLUSION

Table 4 summarises the main criteria which were emphasised at each of the four stages of the review process,[38] and includes also the solutions which were most dominant at each stage. As has been argued, although the veneer of rationality continued throughout the process in the way the Commission's reports were presented, it was only at Stage 1 that there was a serious attempt to follow the logic of the rational model, and even this attempt was fraught with flaws, inconsistencies and misjudgments. By Stage 2 it appeared as though political logic had taken over; the solution had been decided and the LGCs had now to find a way of interpreting the evidence to justify a pre-ordained solution – a role of symbolic legitimation of politically expedient government objectives.[39] That solution was not in fact delivered at Stage 3, although by then it was by no means certain that the government wanted it anyway.[40]

Taken as a whole, the LGR process does exhibit many of the features of the 'garbage can' model – contradictory ill-defined and confused goals, lack of understanding as to how to achieve the goals, fluid participation with policy makers drifting in and out of the debate, and in general terms 'a collection of choices looking for problems ... solutions looking for issues to which they might be an answer, and decision-makers looking for work'.[41] But rationality is always 'bounded' and there is a plausible argument that suggests that, in developing an exit strategy from an increasingly impossible political situation, the LGC were operating a more coherent and effective strategy then appeared at the time to be the case. By early 1994, there was scepticism within the LGC about the justification for 'intermediate unitary solutions'.[42] The LGC had agreed with the government that the search for such solutions was a priority and presumably felt that they had to continue to express this view – at least in public and in discussions with local authorities. The High Court judgment of January 1994, however, legitimised the ultimate recommendation of *status quo* solutions by the LGC. By ensuring there was a preponderance of intermediate unitary recommendations in the summer of 1994, they formally met the requirements of the political context. By signalling the emphasis that would be placed on public preference as a final criteria for decisions, they paved the way for a predominance of *status quo* or hybrid recommendations at the final stage. By then it was apparent that a limited change scenario suited the government. But because that was not their public agenda, a sacrificial scapegoat was required, in the person of Sir John Banham. Seen from this perspective the LGC and its chair, although by no means a model commission in process terms, actually proved to be quite astute politically!

TABLE 4
THE JAXTAPOSITION OF CRITERIA AND SOLUTIONS

	Stage 1	Stage 2	Stage 3	Stage 4 (Cooksey Commission)
Key criteria used (in priority order)	Potential for savings	Avoidance of costs	Public preference	Patterns of life and work (centrality)
	Community identity	Public preference	Avoidance of costs	Public opinion
	Service effectiveness (selected)	Community identity		
	Accountability (joint arrangements)			
Preferred solutions (in priority order)	Large unitary	Intermediate unitary	Status quo (or hybrid)	Status quo or hybrid
	Intermediate unitary hybrid)	Status quo (or unitary	Intermediate	

NOTES

1. See, for example, S. Leach and G. Stoker (eds.), *The Local Government Review in England 1991–96* Special Issue of *Public Administration,* Vol.75 No.3 (Spring 1997); S. Leach, 'The Strange Case of the Local Government Review', in J. Stewart and G. Stoker (eds.), *Local Government in the 1990s* (Macmillan, 1995): R. Wendt, *The Last Word: Reflections on the Local Government Review* (London: Association of County Councils, 1997).
2. See, for example, D. Wilson, 'The Local Government Commission: Examining the

Consultative Process', *Public Administration* Vol.74 No.2 (1996), pp.199–219; the articles by G. Stoker, S. Cope, M. Bailey and R. Atkinson and M. Stott in Leach and Stoker (eds.), op. cit.; and S. Leach, 'Local Government Reorganisation: A Test Case' and 'Scenarios for Change', in S. Leach, H. Davis and associates, *Enabling or Disabling Local Government* (Open University Press, 1996).

3. See, for example, S. Leach, 'The Local Government Review: An Interorganisation Perspective', in Leach and Stoker (eds.), op. cit., and the overview article by S. Leach and G. Stoker, 'Understanding The Local Government Review; A Retrospective Analysis', ibid.

4. M. Clarke, *A Local Government Perspective*, Address to the Joint Local Authority Association Conference in the Future of Local Government, July, 1993.

5. See G. Stoker, 'Introduction to Local Government Reorganisation as a Garbage Can Process', and S. Leach, 'Local Government Reorganisation in England', *Local Government Policy Making*, Vol.19, No.4 (1993); and also S. Leach, 'The Local Government Review: From Vision to Damage Limitation', *Politics Review*, Vol.5, No.3 (1996).

6. Cf. the experience of the Widdcombe Committee, 1985–86 in the development of its report in 'The Conduct of Local Authority Business' (cmnd 9797, HMSO, 1996).

7. See Leach, 'Local Government Reorganisation in England', p.30.

8. See M. Cohen, J. March and J. Olsen, 'A Garbage Can Model of Organisational Choice', *Administrative Science Quarterly* (1972), pp.1–25.

9. See S. Leach, *The Local Government Review: A Crisis of Credibility* (European Policy Forum, London, 1993).

10. See S. Leach, *Local Government Reorganisation: A Test Case*, in Leach, Davis and associates, op. cit., p.51.

11. Namely, Cheshire, Shropshire, Cambridgeshire, Kent and Lones.

12. See Leach, *The Local Government Review: A Crisis of Credibility*, p.3.

13. See, especially, T. Travers, G. Jones and J. Burnham, *The Impact of Population Size on Local Authority Costs and Effectiveness* (York: Joseph Rowntree Foundation, 1993).

14. Local Government Commission for England (LGCE), *The Future Local Government of Derbyshire* (1993), p.34.

15. See C. Game, 'Unprecedented in Local Government Terms – The Local Government Commission's Public Consultation Programme', *Public Administration*, Vol.75, No.1 (1997), pp.68–74.

16. LGCE, *The Future Local Government of Cleveland and Durham* (1993), p.35.

17. LGCE, *The Future Local Government of Derbyshire*, pp.23–4.

18. Ibid., pp.25–6: 'joint working is assisted when local authority boundaries are matched by those of other public sector bodies, especially district health authorities and training and enterprise councils.'

19. Ibid., p.26.

20. LGCE, *The Future Local Government of Cleveland and Durham*, p.30.

21. LGCE, *The Future of Local Government from the Humber to the Wash* (1993), p.64.

22. Ibid., p.80. Compare LGCE, *The Future Local Government of Cleveland and Durham*, p.3: 'the past record of existing cultures – good or bad – is of no relevance to the commission's examination'.

23. See, for example, LGCE, *The Local Government of Derbyshire*, pp.24–5.

24. See, for example, LGCE, *The Future of Local Government North of the Humber* (1993), p.36 (where the argument for boundary extensions of Hull is dismissed) and pp.40–41 (where the argument for boundary extensions to York is accepted).

25. DOE, *Draft Revised Policy Guidance to the Local Government Commission* (1993), p.1.

26. Ibid., pp.2–3.

27. DOE Press Release, 10 Oct. 1993.

28. Sir John Banham, Letter to Secretary of State for the Environment, 19 Oct. 1993.

29. Martin Easteal, address to ADC Conference, 18 Oct. 1993.

30. Lincolnshire, Gloucestershire, Durham and Derbyshire.

31. In the event, the proposed intermediate unitary solutions which were agreed by all (or most) of the districts in a county were widely ignored by the Commission.

32. LGCE, *The Future Local Government of Cheshire: Draft Recommendations* (HMSO, 1994), p.28.
33. See M. Chisholm, *Independence Under Stress, Public Administration,* Vol.75, No.1 (1997), pp.102–3.
34. See, for example, S. Leach and G. Stoker, 'Understanding The Local Government Review: A Retrospective Analysis', *Public Administration,* Vol.75, No.1 (1997).
35. See, for example, LGCE, *The Future Local Government of Avon, Gloucestershire and Somerset* (1993), pp.13–14.
36. LGCE, *The 1995 Review of 21 Districts* in *England* (HMSO, 1995), p.20.
37. LGCE, *The Review of 21 Districts in England,* p.22.
38. Stage 4 covers the Cooksey Commission deliberations.
39. See S. Leach, 'The Strange Case of the Local Government Review', in Stewart and Stoker, *Local Government in the 1990s,* p.67.
40. See Leach and Stoker, 'Understanding the Local Government Review'.
41. Cohen *et al.,* 'A Garbage Can Model of Organisational Choice'.
42. See M. Chisholm, 'Independence Under Stress', *Public Administration,* Vol.75, No.1 (1997), p.102.

The New Public Management and the Local Government Review

ROBERT LEACH AND NEIL BARNETT

INTRODUCTION

. This article seeks to relate the review of English local government undertaken by the Banham Commission from 1992 to 1995 to the New Public Management. After a brief critical evaluation which highlights some of the tensions and ambiguities associated with the New Public Management, its specific applications to local government and its implications for structure are explored. It is argued that, although there were good reasons for expecting the New Public Management to loom large in recommendations for a new structure, and although this was the early expectation of all the main participants in the review process, in practice its relevance steadily declined, and its impact on the final outcome was almost negligible. In this it presents a marked contrast with recent changes in the structure of the civil service and National Health Service. The reasons for this lack of relevance are examined in terms of shortcomings in the review process, but more fundamentally to ambiguities in interpretations of the New Public Management.

THE NEW PUBLIC MANAGEMENT

The New Public Management has become a widely, although not universally, accepted term to describe the introduction of new techniques, concepts and principles to the management of all parts of the public sector in almost all Western countries from the 1980s onwards. Its key elements have been variously described.[1] They are generally taken to include:

- a managerial culture which reflects private sector norms and practices rather than those of traditional public administration;
- more managerial delegation, decentralisation, and organisational disaggregation;
- an emphasis on economy, efficiency, and effectiveness;

Robert Leach and Neil Barnett, Leeds Business School, Leeds Metropolitan University

- performance measurement, standards and targets;
- flexibility of pay and conditions, sometimes including performance-related pay;
- a greater emphasis on customer choice and service quality;
- the contracting out of some service provision to the private sector;
- the promotion of contractual relationships within the public sector – and the separation of purchaser and provider (or client and contractor) roles;
- the promotion of competition, markets and quasi-markets within the public sector.

Most attempts to provide a 'shopping list' of the elements or characteristics of the New Public Management include the above, although the precise wording, and still more the order, varies considerably, which may subtly alter the emphasis. Further explanations often give special prominence to one term or concept, which, it is stated or inferred, the New Public Management is 'really about'. Thus it is sometimes suggested that the New Public Management is essentially about 'consumerism' or 'markets' or 'privatisation' or simply 'cutting costs'.[2]

So, although the New Public Management is generally reckoned to be a useful shorthand term to describe recent developments across countries, policy areas and levels of government, it is an imprecise term, with some ambiguities. There is clearly some potential tension between its perceived elements. Maintaining or improving quality, meeting standards and satisfying customers may conflict with economy and efficiency, particularly if these are interpreted in terms of cost cutting. There are also problems in defining and applying core values. Thus, for example, competition may be encouraged in very different ways, some of which might involve market testing, or internal markets, but which may not necessarily involve markets at all.[3] Delegation and decentralisation may also take very different forms.[4] In practice, the New Public Management often appears to involve both centralisation and decentralisation. While operational management is decentralised, strategic planning and finance may be more subject to central control. Even the rejection of old, traditional bureaucratic norms and practices, sometimes perceived as a defining characteristic of the New Public Management, is by no means total and unambiguous. Thus Hoggett[5] has pointed to the essentially paradoxical nature of the New Public Management, involving hybrid organisational forms which combine elements of innovation with a number of traditional bureaucratic control mechanisms.

Explanations for the development of the New Public Management focus on both the context in which it has developed and its intellectual derivation. Hood,[6] for example, points to a context of fiscal crisis and resource constraints, coupled with changing technologies, social pressures and increased consumer demands on public services, all intensifying pressures for efficiency savings. A similar analysis is provided by Kirkpatrick and Lucio.[7] Other broader contextual explanations focus on post-Fordism, post-industrialism and post-modernism, implying a shift from the large scale, bureaucratic and paternalist mass provision of universal and uniform services to smaller scale, more flexible responses to the needs and requirements of individual consumers in a post-bureaucratic environment.

In terms of ideas the New Public Management does not reflect a single coherent theory but is derived from a variety of sources. Hood interpreted the New Public Management as 'a marriage of two different streams of ideas' involving 'the new institutional economics' and 'the latest of a set of successive waves of business-type managerialism'.[8] Aucoin similarly saw the New Public Management as a combination of public choice theory and managerialist thinking. He went on to argue that this twin derivation involved some tension, between closer control of public sector bureaucrats implied by public choice theory, and the 'managerialist' emphasis on delegation and 'freedom to manage'.[9]

Public choice theory has become associated with the New Right, and the private sector origins of some of the fashionable managerial ideas also suggest that provenance of the New Public Management is ideologically right wing or neo-liberal. Moreover, in the United Kingdom the introduction of the New Public Management has been widely perceived as an essentially top-down process, involving the implementation of a Thatcherite Conservative political agenda. However, it is sometimes argued that the New Public Management is essentially politically neutral, concerned with the efficient administration of policy. Interpretations of the New Public Management which stress its origins in managerial and organisational theory point to new forms of organisational control, applicable across the political spectrum.[10] Elsewhere in the world it has been introduced by left or centre-left governments, suggesting a response to changing conditions rather than a reflection of a specific political ideology.

The New Public Management is thus 'multi-faceted' and 'multi-valued'.[11] To some critics, its elastic character is reminiscent of the 'emperor's new clothes'. Its all-inclusive nature means it has the potential to stand for everything and nothing.[12] To others its inherent flexibility is seen as an advantage, allowing scope for actors within the public sector to mediate and shape the nature of the reform programme. Thus it has been argued that mediation at local level has produced a diversity of organisational forms and outcomes.[13] This is particularly relevant to the manifestation of the New Public Management in UK local government.

THE NEW PUBLIC MANAGEMENT AND LOCAL GOVERNMENT

The New Public Management is generally assumed to have a universal relevance, across countries, services, policy areas and levels of government. Therefore it should be manifest in local government as well as in other parts of the United Kingdom political system. Indeed, this has been widely acknowledged, although there has been an understandable reluctance to employ the term among some of those, who, like John Stewart, have been at the cutting edge of management reform in local government for over 30 years, the more especially because its claimed novelty implies a blanket repudiation of a past with which they have been closely associated. Thus they would argue that elements of this older reform agenda have been incorporated into the package of ideas associated with the New Public Management. Moreover, that package, involving a mishmash of ideas, old, new, borrowed and blue, does not warrant unqualified endorsement.[14]

Even so, it is certainly not difficult to interpret many key changes in UK local government in terms of the New Public Management. These include the privatisation of some local authority housing and the encouragement of alternative forms of public provision, the changes in audit and the emphasis on the '3 Es', the deregulation of public transport, the introduction of compulsory competitive tendering, and the reforms in the provision of education services. All these developments are broadly comparable with changes in other parts of the UK public sector, and indeed with government elsewhere.

Moreover, there can be little doubt that the organisational culture of local government has been significantly transformed from that which prevailed in the early 1970s. Then the preoccupation was with the realisation of economies of scale, and with the introduction of corporate management, involving authority-wide planning, and the integration of separate professions, services and departments into a corporate entity, strengthened by new strong central co-ordinating institutions. Both the language and the underlying assumptions are very different today. Instead of economies of scale, the emphasis now is on disaggregation, downsizing and flexibility. Instead of integration and co-ordination, the stress today is on competition and consumer choice. Instead of strong centralised officer and member leadership, there is instead a drive towards delegation and decentralisation. The more ambitious forms of corporate planning advocated in the 1970s are no longer viable in the new environment. Both members and officers now operate in a very different climate.

Yet if the New Public Management in local government clearly resembles aspects of its application elsewhere, in the civil service and the National Health Service, it also has distinctive features. Thus there are some significant differences in terms of origins, the derivation of ideas, key concepts and application.

For example, while it is generally argued that the New Public Management has been introduced in the UK from the top downwards, this is not wholly the case with local government. Certainly many of the changes commonly associated with the New Public Management have been imposed from the centre, and only reluctantly accepted by local authorities. This would be true of CCT and the bulk of the changes in housing, public transport and education (although even here the experiments of New Right local authorities like Wandsworth paved the way). Yet there have also been fertile experiments in promoting accessibility, decentralisation, citizen involvement and customer care by a range of local authorities. Recommendations from the Audit Commission, commonly associated with central control, often reflect best practice by innovatory local authorities, who have pioneered new approaches to performance review and quality assurance. Thus much of management change in local government has been internally generated. Hoggett suggests that there has been a 'process of management learning which moves backwards and forwards between local and central levels of government'.[15]

This suggests that the intellectual provenance of the New Public Management in local government is mixed. Certainly some of it derives from fashionable private sector management thinking, and some of it reflects New Right ideas, and more specifically public choice theory (although not very consistently). But other initiatives in local government which appear compatible with the New Public Management have a very different ideological inspiration. Elements of both the New Urban Left and the Liberal Democrats have promoted access, decentralisation and citizen empowerment, in the name of local socialism or community politics.

One concept particularly associated with the New Public Management in local government which has less obvious relevance to other parts of the public sector is that of the enabling authority.[16] It is a concept which also reflects the ambiguous intellectual ancestry of much management change in local government. While often attributed to the New Right orthodoxy of Nicholas Ridley,[17] it is also closely associated with the very different ideas of Clarke and Stewart,[18] and can be traced back to Stewart's earlier collaboration with George Jones in 1983: 'The Case for Local Government'.[19] Unsurprisingly, in view of its mixed provenance, the concept of enabling has been very variously interpreted, in terms of residual enabling, market enabling and community enabling, suggesting very different underlying values and strongly contrasting implications for the operations of local government generally,[20] and contestable implications for structure.

THE NEW PUBLIC MANAGEMENT AND LOCAL GOVERNMENT STRUCTURE

No clear causal relationship necessarily exists between internal management reforms and changes in local government structure, although the two have often been associated. Thus in the 1960s it was widely hoped that structural reform would be accompanied by improvements in the management and conduct of local government business. Sir John Maud, who presided over the Committee on the Management of the Local Government which reported in 1967, as Lord Redcliffe-Maud went on to chair the Royal Commission on Local Government in England.[21] The long drawn-out debate over reorganisation which culminated in the 1972 Act in turn spawned the Bains Report on the management of the new authorities.[22] There were, in effect, two parallel but connected reform agendas, one to modernise the areas and boundaries of local authorities, the other to achieve a more corporate approach amounting (for some more enthusiastic advocates) to a management revolution.

The introduction of the New Public Management into local government from the 1980s onwards was not, however, at first associated with major structural reform. This is in marked contrast with what has happened elsewhere in the public sector. Management reforms in the health service have been linked with a progressive simplification of the post-1974 three-tier structure of health authorities, coupled with the proliferation of a host of new micro-agencies competing in an internal market. In the civil service the New Public Management has involved the replacement of the old centralised, hierarchical and bureaucratic structures in traditional government departments by Next Steps Agencies. Moreover, managerial delegation has often been associated with significant geographical decentralisation.

There were initially no commensurate changes to the structure of local government. The Thatcher government's abolition of the GLC and Metropolitan County Councils took place before the new management revolution was properly under way, and was not justified in terms of the need for managerial change. There was no apparent threat to the rest of the two-tier system. Indeed the introduction of the NPM into local government did not at first seem to have clear implications for structure. The early parts of the NPM agenda, unlike the corporate management agenda of the late 1960s and early 1970s, was not about broad strategy, but more about micro-level changes, involving increased managerial and financial delegation. Much of this could apparently be achieved without fundamental structural change.

Yet within the shell of the continuing two-tier system of local government the New Public Management increasingly involved massive changes in functions, methods of operating and internal organisation. On the one hand, there was an effective transfer of some formal functions and many more operational responsibilities away from local government to a host of quangos, micro-agencies, voluntary organisations and the private sector. On the other hand, the imposition of competitive tendering, deregulation and delegation created a range of virtually autonomous management units operating under the local government umbrella. All this clearly might have some implications for the territorial organisation of local government. Was there still enough for local government to do to warrant the continued existence of two operational tiers? Did the new emphasis on the enabling role undermine traditional assumptions concerning the relationship between authority size and efficiency?

If these possible implications for structure were not initially appreciated it was partly because, as compared with the management revolution in the civil service and NHS, there was less coherent sense of direction behind the various management changes in local government. There, indeed, the very identification of the phenomenon of the NPM involves some *post hoc* rationalisation of a series of initially disconnected initiatives, with diverse origins and ideological ancestries. There was never, it seems, a Thatcher or Major master plan for local government, more a series of *ad hoc* responses to specific policy problems, which only cumulatively and retrospectively added up to a management revolution, which might, just possibly, have implications for structure.

Yet briefly it seemed that something approaching a master plan for local government was to be prepared. In the spring of 1991 the Major government issued three consultation papers, on the finance, management and structure of local government.[23] This implied a rather more co-ordinated approach than was customary with central government initiatives towards local government, inspired by a Minister, Michael Heseltine, with his own distinctive agenda.

In practice, it soon became clear that there were very different timetables for the three policy areas covered by the consultation papers. Political exigencies required a quick fix on finance before the 1992 General Election, the programme for structural change was planned to take place over several years, while prospects for some of the projected reforms of internal management receded with Heseltine's departure from the DoE.

Even so, it appeared at first that structural reform was strongly predicated on the new ideas on management in local government. The 1991 White Paper 'Competing for Quality' roundly declared: 'The Government's model for local government in the 1990s and into the 21st century is that of the enabling authority.'[24] The 1991 DoE Consultation Paper on structure also emphasised the importance of the enabling role, arguing that 'the changing role of local government has significantly altered the presumption, widely current in the years leading up to the Local Government Act 1972 that there is an ideal size of authority for the most efficient delivery of services'. Thus a new structure was required for a new role.

Yet the ensuing local government review was complicated from the start by other objectives. The Local Government Act 1992 which established the Local Government Commission for England required it to make recommendations (i) to reflect the identities and interests of local communities and (ii) to secure effective and convenient local government.

These objectives were supplemented by a strong direction towards unitary authorities. While this could be seen as a means to the ends of the two primary objectives cited above, it soon became clear that this was to be one of the main criteria by which the government would judge the Commisssion's recommendations.

The requirement to reconcile managerial efficiency on the one hand with community identity on the other had been problematic issues with past proposed and actual reforms of local government structure. The 1966–69 Redcliffe-Maud Royal Commission had concluded, on the basis of its research findings, that most people identified with areas far too small for efficient local government. In consequence, community identity was effectively sacrificed to efficiency in its predominantly unitary system. By contrast, the difficulty of devising unitary authorities to ensure both efficient service delivery and government close to the people helped persuade Heath's Conservative government of the merits of a two-tier system.

However, superficially it appeared that the New Public Management might be rather more compatible with community interests. This was partly for the essentially negative reason that the shift from providing to enabling apparently removed some of the assumed benefits of larger authority size. Yet also, and more positively, parts of the New Public Management agenda, particularly closeness to the customer and organisational disaggregation, could be interpreted in terms of community values. Thus there was no longer necessarily a trade off between efficiency and community. Both, it could be argued, now required accessibility, delegation and decentralisation.

THE NEW PUBLIC MANAGEMENT AND THE PROGRESS OF THE LOCAL GOVERNMENT REVIEW

The Local Government Commission for England initially seemed to attach as much importance as the government to 'the concept of the enabling authority and other management improvements' both in its 1993 Progress Report[25] and in early draft reports. 'The role of the local authority as a

purchaser of services is a key consideration for the Commission in its wish
to establish a local government structure which will meet the needs of the
next century'.[26] The Commission's Progress Report also spelt out in more
detail how it interpreted the enabling role, and in so doing linked the
management changes in local government with those elsewhere in the
public sector, with further references to private sector inspiration.

> The changes in management are generally in the same direction: in
> central government, the health service and local authorities. The
> principal body allocates resources, sets standards and monitors
> performance, while devolving day-to-day management responsibility
> to freestanding units or to external contractors. This process is
> continuing in local government, and many of the changes are still
> working their way through the system. The Commission believes that
> local government in the year 2000 and beyond will be very different
> from now, even if no more changes to service provision are made, and
> that many new unitary authorities will be as different from their
> predecessors as so many British companies are today from their
> predecessors of ten years ago. (Progress Report, chapter 2, para. 33)

The report went on to state that 'the Commission also believes that the
introduction of new unitary structures can provide an enhanced opportunity
for enabling practices', without spelling out the grounds for this belief.
Nevertheless, the implications were clear; the changes in management were
to be a key factor in determining the new structure.

To judge from their submissions to the Banham Commission, local
authorities thought so too, particularly those involved in the first tranche of
the review process. Encouraged by the Association of District Councils to
aspire to unitary status, shire districts sought to demonstrate their capacity
to assume responsibility for all local government services by asserting their
new management credentials. Counties, faced with an initially difficult
defensive action, employed similar terminology to establish their flexibility
and closeness to the customer. The same phrases and concepts reappear
through most of the early glossy literature produced by authorities of
different types, sizes and from different areas, reflecting common
assumptions, as well as the guidance received from their associations, and
advice from a limited number of consultants.

Thus almost all authorities stressed their awareness of the new
managerial environment and their customer care credentials. Central to the
case of smaller districts in particular was that they could be 'closer to the
people' and more responsive to local needs. Small size was presented as a
positive advantage in terms of local accessibility, decentralisation and
delegation. Claimed existing commitments to customer care would be

extended to new unitary responsibilities, which would allow a more integrated, customer-related service provision, through 'one stop shops'. Their more local perspective would assist a flexible approach, while at the same time offering more co-ordination between functions such as housing and social services, for which some districts like York proposed a single integrated department.

The counties, by contrast, emphasised that the scale of their operations enabled them to target resources for customers more effectively, while their established partnership and joint working arrangements with other statutory and voluntary bodies facilitated integrated customer care, interpreted essentially as a capacity to deliver. They also stressed their own decentralising credentials with reference to hundreds of local access points to services, coupled with a claimed record of established consultation and partnership with town and parish councils.

Councils of all types claimed to have reduced bureaucracy and introduced 'leaner' and 'flatter' organisational structures. Thus Derby City established its new managerialist credentials by contrasting its old 1980s 'traditional' structure involving a 'large number' of professional Chief Officers, with its new five multi-functional departments incorporating business units, cost centres and trading accounts for in-house professional services.

Central to the submissions of both counties and districts was the concept of enabling, variously interpreted. Some smaller districts pursuing unitary status saw enabling largely in terms of contracting out, to imply a residual enabler role. This was crucial to their case, to combat the view that unitary authorities based on existing district boundaries would not generally be large enough to provide all services in-house. Enabling, it was confidently anticipated, would allow smaller authorities to procure and deliver effective and efficient services using a variety of sources. Authorities thus stressed their enabling credentials and their commitment to the contracting environment. High Peak Borough Council claimed they had 'built up a culture in the organisation of enabling, or rather of depending upon external service provision' long before the term 'enabling' had come into common use.

This view of enabling in particular allowed smaller authorities to claim they could cope with anticipated unitary responsibilities for education and social services. Thus it was argued that the 1988 Education Act had removed the assumption that LEAs must be large, self-sufficient providers of services. Instead, they would need to market support services to schools and act as brokers between locally managed schools. Social service provision would require the commissioning of care services from a variety of sources, a 'mixed economy' of care which would involve the public, private and voluntary sectors. The purchaser/provider relationship would enable councils to purchase specialist services from other authorities with a particular expertise, without necessitating too many cumbersome joint arrangements.

Some districts and most counties interpreted enabling more broadly, to imply a strategic capacity to manage and influence the broad development of their area. Here a more proactive role was assumed for the local authority, which would play a lead role in creating partnerships with other players in the locality, including business organisations, the voluntary sector and other statutory bodies to achieve agreed policy objectives, particularly in the area of economic regeneration. The counties naturally stressed the advantages of size. The larger authority would be in a position of greater influence and clout and be much more likely to develop the strategic partnerships required to attract international business locations, and to compete for government and European Union grant aid.

Councils' submissions to Banham of course largely reflected what it was assumed the Commission, and ultimately the government, wanted to hear. Thus most authorities seemed to endorse, with every indication of enthusiasm, changes in functions and management innovations which a good many had earlier resisted. They did this because the 'rules of the game', as they were initially perceived, required it. The future lay with the New Public Management. Only authorities with a commitment to the values and processes of the new managerialism could expect to survive and thrive in the new local government system.

THE NEW PUBLIC MANAGEMENT AND THE OUTCOME OF THE LOCAL GOVERNMENT REVIEW

Although all the major participants in the review process – the government, the Commission, the local authorities and their associations – behaved, at least in the early stages, as if they believed that new management ideas would be an important determinant of recommendations on changes to structure, the influence of those ideas on the final outcome would appear to have been almost negligible. Instead of the envisaged modernised local government structure to meet the management needs of the twenty-first century, a new structure emerged strangely reminiscent of that which prevailed before 1974, with unitary authorities only in the larger urban centres, and two-thirds of the country covered by two-tier local government. While this may be justifiable on other grounds, it has little apparent relevance to the new management thinking which loomed so large in the early stages of the review.

Whereas the Redcliffe-Maud Commission has sometimes been accused of sacrificing considerations of community to unproved assumptions over efficiency, the Banham Commission progressively attached greater importance to the community dimension, and relatively neglected efficiency. Thus the recommendations of the Commission increasingly reflected the evidence on community, interpreted through the MORI surveys, almost exclusively in terms of felt identity or affective community, and on public reaction to its earlier draft proposals, As a consequence, it steadily abandoned its earlier strong endorsement of unitary authorities, evident in most of its early draft recommendations and in its Progress Report, bowing to an apparent public preference for the maintenance of the two-tier *status quo* over much of England.

This arguably had implications for the new managerialism also, as in its Progress Report the Commission had expressed its belief that the introduction of new unitary structures would assist the move towards enabling and new management practices. The change in approach by the Commission is most clearly evident from a comparison between the 1993 Progress Report and the report produced by the Commission before its membership was remodelled in March 1995.[27] In the Progress Report the Commission echoed the strong preference of the government for unitary authorities, while in the final report the argument is more detached and even-handed, concluding that 'the relative merits of unitary and two-tier structures was not a matter of simple objective measurement. Both models offer distinct advantages and disadvantages for the performance of different local government functions' (para. 38).

The differences between the two reports are even more starkly apparent with regard to the enabling role and other new management ideas. Considerable significance had been attached to the notion of the enabling authority in the Progress Report (paras. 31–46) with the clear implication that this would be an important consideration in recommending changes to structure. In the final report it was scarcely mentioned. Although the changes in local government's functions, service delivery and managerial philosophies are briefly summarised, along with many other changes in 'the contemporary context of local government's operations', no conclusions are derived from the discussion. When the report goes on to consider 'effective and convenient local government', one of the original twin objectives of reform, the agenda of the New Public Management is conspicuous by its absence. Instead there is an analysis of the problems in administering particular services, which is heavily dependent on submissions from national and regional bodies, with some of which the Commission had a statutory obligation to consult.

Many of these submissions stressed the importance of a strategic view, concerns over specialist services, and 'an anxiety that any division of existing county services would be detrimental' (para. 75). Thus the Society of Education Officers and the Secondary Heads Association both considered that 'sub-county unitary authorities would be unable to provide the requisite expertise and range of professional services' (para. 78). Various transport bodies were concerned that 'a wide strategic view' was necessary for highways and transportation functions, and that 'smaller unitary authorities relying on joint arrangements would not be able to do this' (para. 89), while 'organisations promoting public transport were concerned that district-based unitary authorities would not wish or be able to maintain subsidised bus and rail routes in rural areas' (para. 90). On library services, 'respondents expressed a concern that a move to unitary authorities would make it harder to maintain and improve the quality of library services' (para. 92). On nature conservation and countryside interests the Countryside Commission 'reflected a general wish to avoid unnecessary fragmentation of services' and 'the uncertain effects of change on discretionary services' (para. 95). The Association of Directors of Social Services 'believed that, in general, new unitary authorities in shire England with a population of less than 200,000 were likely to experience considerable difficulties' (para. 99). Similar points were made about a number of more specialist services. Thus the National Council on Archives argued that the archive service 'required units which were large enough to cope with a range of specialisms, sustain economies of scale and prevent fragmentation of collections' (para. 107).

Such submissions were summarised by the Commission without comment, and without critical scrutiny of claims made by organisations with considerable experience of specific services but also reflecting their own vested interests. The whole chapter owed little to the New Public Management, but rather more to the values of traditional public administration, with an emphasis on efficiency of service delivery, consistency, integration, co-ordination, and economies of scale.

Indeed, for all the lip service paid to the new managerialism in the early stages of the review, in retrospect it was some fairly well-established traditional administrative principles which seem to have underpinned the Commission's work, and, indeed, as far as it can be discerned, the government's own thinking. The financial costings model, which loomed large in the early stages of the review process, in practice ruled out the unitary district model for which the Association of District Councils had optimistically encouraged its members to strive. This became obvious as the Commission swiftly rejected unitary authorities based on existing district boundaries in Derbyshire, County Durham, North Yorkshire and Humberside. Despite the routine insistence that there was no blueprint and no assumptions about the size of unitary authorities, such size criteria soon emerged in the form of a guide population range of 150,000–250,000. No attempt was ever made to justify these figures, which would seem to have more to do with some fairly crude assumptions over economies of scale, rather than with the enabling role or the New Public Management, unless the latter is cynically interpreted in terms of simple cost cutting. Although these figures were described as 'indicative' rather than 'prescriptive' they bore a not entirely coincidental resemblance to the break-even point in the costings model, which generally involved roughly halving the number of existing authorities. The Commission itself drew some instructive comparisons with the government's own proposals for Wales and Scotland (Progress Report, para. 4).

In so far as the Commission subsequently declined to satisfy government expectations, culminating in the sacking of Sir John Banham and the remodelling of the Commission in 1995, this had little to do with any perception of efficiency, whether related to old-style public administration or the New Public Management. Quite simply, the whole management dimension became progressively less important, as the Commission increasingly relied on the evidence of community identity from the MORI surveys, and the results of their own public consultation exercises. Reluctantly, the Commission came to the conclusion that while there was considerable evidence that the public were attracted to the idea of unitary authorities in the abstract, they did not like the particular unitary solutions proposed over much of the country. Thus most of their final reports recommended the continuation of the two-tier *status quo*. In this they obstinately persisted, even when instructed to think again by the government. The final report of the original Commission provided some *post hoc* rationalisation for this outcome, but no real justification in terms of the changing role and changing management culture of local government.

PROBLEMS IN APPLYING THE NEW PUBLIC MANAGEMENT TO LOCAL GOVERNMENT REORGANISATION

Could it have been otherwise? Might the theory and practice of the New Public Management provide the basis for a principled reorganisation to meet the requirements of local government in the twenty-first century?

Some criticism might be levelled at the conduct of the review. It might conceivably have helped had the Commission undertaken some research into the operations of the new management ideas on local government in the United Kingdom and abroad. As both the government and the Commission noted, the changes in the management and delivery of services suggested that the old assumptions of economies of scale in service delivery might no longer be relevant (even if those old assumptions had never been clearly validated by empirical research). As the changes are relatively recent and still on-going, the evidence is scanty. A 1993 Rowntree Foundation report[28] found no consistent relationship between scale and efficiency either in its survey of English authorities or in its brief review of local government abroad. While it was recognised that the shift to enabling had significant implications for the debate, the contrasting arguments of rival local authority associations were merely summarised and subjected to some critical scrutiny, with no clear conclusions. The report found evidence for the existence of diseconomies of scale in some services, but also 'clear commercial evidence that large purchasers can achieve lower tender prices than smaller ones'. Significantly, it was also noted that 'even the move towards the "enabling authority" does not appear yet to have provided many examples of authorities grouping together to buy services' (p.17). The Local Government Commission might have attempted to build on this research, with particular reference to the shift towards enabling, but ducked the issue.

However, it is possible that even if such research had been undertaken by the Commission, it would have proved no more conclusive than earlier work. Meaningful measurement depends on clear definitions of core concepts. Measuring the impact of the New Public Management is rendered more difficult by the ambiguities surrounding its very nature. Nor does it help if the New Public Management is defined for local government purposes in terms of the 'enabling role', because there are considerable differences in the interpretation of that role. Distinctions have been drawn between three ideal types of enabling authority, the residual enabling authority, the market-oriented enabler and the community-oriented enabling authority.[29] Each have very different implications for the role of local government. Tentative efforts have been made to tease out very different structural implications from different models of enabling.[30] The conclusions are suggestive, if still highly contentious, but they underline how difficult it is to 'read off' a particular structure from assumptions about the management of local government.

Different interpretations of core concepts associated with the New Public Management and the enabling role reflect more fundamental differences over the real role and purpose of local government. The common terminology of the New Public Management has sometimes obscured basic disagreements over what local government is, or should be, for. This was, for some commentators, the missing element at the heart of the local government review.[31] How could the Commission arrive at sensible recommendations for changes in structure without clear guidance from the government on the future role of local government? It is a fair point. Although a government view of the role of local government can be discerned or inferred from various sources, it was never consistently promoted, which perhaps reflects differences, only half articulated, within government, and no clear coherent vision. Ambiguities over ultimate objectives were effectively compounded by different interpretations of the New Public Management and the key concept of enabling. All sides could make use of the same terminology to promote their own interests and their own different perceptions of the future role of local government. To that extent the New Public Management obfuscated rather than clarified the issues. Yet ambiguity often serves political purposes. The absence of clear direction enabled different interests within and outside local government to attempt to influence the agenda and remake the rules of the game. If the outcome of the local government review was a messy compromise which hardly satisfied anyone, that too might be seen as a characteristic consequence of a pluralist decision-making process. However, it is at least debatable whether a clearer government conception of the role of local government, consistently applied, would have produced a more generally acceptable outcome.

NOTES

1. See, for example, C. Hood, 'A Public Management for All Seasons', *Public Administration*, Vol.69 (Spring 1991); J. Stewart and K. Walsh, 'Change in the Management of Public Services', *Public Administration*, Vol.70 (Winter 1992), D. Farnham and S. Horton, *Managing the New Public Services* (London: Macmillan, 1993); P. Dunleavy, 'The Globalization of Public Services Production, *Public Policy and Administration*, Vol.9, No.2 (1994), pp.36–64; C. Pollitt, 'Justification by Works or Faith? Evaluating the New Public Management', *Evaluation*, Vol.1, pp.133–54.
2. R. Rhodes, 'Introduction', *Public Administration*, Vol.69 (Spring 1991), pp.1–2.
3. R. Common, N. Flynn and E. Mellon, *Managing Public Services: Competition and Decentralisation* (Oxford: Butterworth-Heinemann, 1992).
4. D.R. Burns, R. Hambleton and P. Hoggett, *The Politics of Decentralisation: Reviving Local Democracy* (London: Macmillan, 1994).
5. P. Hoggett, 'New Modes of Control in the Public Service', *Public Administration*, Vol.74, No.1 (Spring 1996).
6. C. Hood, 'A Public Management for All Seasons', *Public Administration*, Vol.69 (Spring 1991), pp.3–19.
7. I. Kirkpatrick and M.M. Lucio, 'Introduction: The Contract State and the Future of Public Management', *Public Administration*, Vol.74 (Spring 1996), pp.1–8.
8. Hood, 'A Public Management for All Seasons', p.5.
9. P. Aucoin, 'Administrative Reform in Public Management: Paradigms, Principles, Paradoxes and Pendulums', *Governance: An International Journal of Policy and Administration*, Vol.3, No.2 (April 1990).
10. P. Hoggett, 'A New Management in the Public Sector?', *Policy and Politics*, Vol.19, No.4 (1991), pp.243–56.
11. Pollitt, 'Justification'.
12. P. Dunleavy and C. Hood, 'From Old Public Administration to New Public Management', *Public Money and Management*, Vol.14, No.3 (1994), pp.9–16.
13. Kirkpatrick and Lucio, 'Introduction', pp.1–8.
14. S. Leach, J. Stewart and K. Walsh, *The Changing Organisation and Management of Local Government* (London: Macmillan, 1994).

15. Hoggett, 'A New Management in the Public Sector?', p.248.
16. R. Brooke, *Managing the Enabling Authority* (Harlow: Longman, 1989).
17. N. Ridley, *The Local Right* (London: Centre for Policy Studies, 1988).
18. M. Clarke and J. Stewart, *The Enabling Council* (Luton: Local Government Training Board, 1988).
19. G. Jones and J. Stewart, *The Case for Local Government* (London: George Allen and Unwin, 1983).
20. Leach, Stewart and Walsh, *The Changing Organisation and Management of Local Government.*
21. Lord Redcliffe-Maud, *Royal Commission on Local Government in England* (London: HMSO, Cmnd 4040, 1969).
22. M. Bains, *The New Local Authorities: Management and Structure* (London: HMSO, 1972).
23. Department of the Environment, *A New Tax for Local Government: Consultation Document*; Department of the Environment, *Competing for Quality – Competiveness in the Provision of Public Services; A Consultation Paper*; The Department of the Environment, *The Structure of Local Government in the United Kingdom: A Consultation Paper* (all London: Department of the Environment, 1991).
24. Her Majesty's Treasury, *Competing for Quality* (London: HMSO, 1991, Cm. 1730).
25. Local Government Commission for England, *Renewing Local Government in the English Shires: A Progress Report* (London: HMSO, 1993).
26. For example, Local Government Commission for England, *Draft Recommendations on the Future Local Government of Derbyshire* (London: Local Government Commission for England, 1993).
27. The Local Government Commission for England, *Renewing Local Government in the English Shires: A Report on the 1992–1995 Structural Review* (London: HMSO, 1995).
28. T. Travers, G. Jones and J. Burnham, *The Impact of Population Size on Local Authority Costs and Effectiveness* (York: Joseph Rowntree Foundation, 1993).
29. Leach, Stewart and Walsh, *The Changing Organisation and Management of Local Government.*
30. D. Wilson and C. Game, *Local Government in the United Kingdom* (London: Macmillan, 1994). See also R. Leach, 'Reorganising for Enabling? Restructuring Local Government for an Altered Role', *Public Policy and Administration*, Vol.9, No.3 (Winter 1994), pp.52–62.
31. S. Leach (ed.), *The Local Government Review: Key Issues and Choices* (Birmingham: Institute of Local Government Studies, 1994).

Public Choice Theory and Local Government Structure: An Evaluation of Reorganisation in Scotland and Wales

GEORGE A. BOYNE

INTRODUCTION

The aims of this paper are to outline a public choice model of local government structure and to compare the new local government systems in Scotland and Wales with this model. In principle, it should be possible to use public choice theory to draw clear conclusions on the relative merits of the old and new structures. The public choice perspective has been developed over a period of 40 years, largely on the basis of economic reasoning which is supposedly characterised by explicit assumptions and deductive rigour. This may be so in the abstract, but it remains to be seen whether public choice theory delivers definite judgements on real changes in local government structure.

A public choice perspective on reorganisation is important for at least three reasons. First, critiques of previous and current structural reforms in the UK have rested largely on 'consolidationist' arguments. These assume that planning and co-ordination are essential to good performance in local government systems.[1] Public choice theory provides a sharply contrasting view that efficiency and responsiveness are enhanced by local government structures based on markets and competition. Regardless of the empirical validity of such arguments, the public choice perspective broadens the debate on reorganisation. As Sharpe comments on the reorganisation debates in the 1960s and 1970s, 'there can be little doubt that the reform process in Britain would have been enriched had the public choice theorists participated'.[2] Secondly, conventional consolidationist arguments on structure are concerned only with fragmentation, that is the number of tiers and number of separate units in each one. Public choice theory focuses not only on fragmentation but also concentration, or the 'market share' of each tier and unit. This element of structure would be missed by an analysis which rested on consolidationist assumptions. Thirdly, public choice theory overlaps with elements of the new right philosophy which has influenced

George A. Boyne, Cardiff Business School

Conservative policies towards the public sector. For example, the structural fragmentation which is central to the public choice model can be regarded as a means of promoting new right values of individualism and choice in local government.[3] It is therefore useful to evaluate the extent to which public choice principles are reflected in the structures which the Conservatives imposed on Scotland and Wales.

It is important to emphasise that the purpose of the paper is to use public choice theory to *evaluate* the new structures rather than to *explain* their adoption.[4] It must also be stressed that the aim of the paper is *not* to argue that local government structures should be based on public choice principles. The questions to be addressed are not normative but positive: does public choice theory offer a clear model of local government structure, and have the Scottish and Welsh local government systems been moved towards this model? The first part of the paper highlights the main public choice arguments on structure, and combines these into a framework which can be applied empirically. The second part examines general criticisms of public choice theory, and evaluates their relevance to specific arguments on local government structure. Part III analyses whether the structural reforms in Scotland and Wales have produced local government systems that are consistent with the public choice model. This attempt to apply public choice theory empirically reveals a number of problems in the theory itself.

PUBLIC CHOICE THEORY AND LOCAL GOVERNMENT STRUCTURE

Although public choice arguments are widespread in the literature on local government in the USA, no comprehensive model of structure has been developed. Rather, numerous theoretical propositions are scattered throughout a variety of sources. The purpose of this section is to fit these pieces into a more coherent mosaic. A different review of the main public choice arguments might produce a slightly different picture, but the general features would almost certainly be similar. It is, nevertheless, worth noting that the framework which is developed here should be regarded as 'a' public choice model rather than 'the' public choice model – the latter simply does not exist.

Authors working in the public choice tradition share two assumptions concerning local government. The first is the *self-interest axiom* which implies that, left to their own devices, policy makers will pursue their private interests rather than the public interest. Secondly, politicians and officials can be redirected towards the public interest if they are constrained by the pressure of *competition*. Public choice theory views local government as an industry in which there are buyers and sellers in the market for local services. The buyers are households and businesses who choose to locate in specific areas and pay for their choices through local taxes; and the sellers are politicians and bureaucrats who either procure or directly provide services for the public.[5] Competition between councils can take two forms. First, geographical competition between authorities in different areas for a share of the market in households and businesses. Second, competition between different tiers of local governments for a share of local tax revenues in the same geographical area. Public choice theory suggests that competition in the local government industry is maximised if three structural characteristics are present. First, a fragmented structure with many units; second, a deconcentrated structure where units have equal market shares; and, third, a flexible structure with low barriers to entry and exit. Each of these characteristics is discussed in more detail below. It should be noted that structural arrangements are not the only influence on competition between councils – levels of central funding and local autonomy are also important.[6] The following discussion of the effects of structure therefore assumes that such variables are held constant.

(a) Fragmentation

This dimension of structure may vary between two extremes. In a 'consolidated' structure all services are provided by a single unit that covers a wide geographical area. In such a single-tier system each authority has a monopoly over all local services and has an extensive spatial monopoly. By contrast, in a fragmented structure, local government is divided into many tiers with many units in each tier. The public choice preference for a fragmented structure is a reaction against the 'conventional' view that large, hierarchial, multi-purpose organisations are the best way to organise local public services.[7] The public choice approach does not completely reject arguments for large units of local government which may be necessary for some services in order to internalise externalities and take advantage of economies of scale.[8] However, it is important to note that scale effects refer to the level of output rather than population size per se, and that economies of scale may be present at the level of 'plants' (for example, a school) rather than at the 'firm' level of a local authority as a whole.[9] In this case, even small authorities may be able to produce services at minimum cost. Moreover, any benefits from economies of scale in large authorities may not be sufficient to compensate for the costs of monopoly.[10]

Tiebout argues that a highly fragmented local government system with many authorities provides a 'market type' solution to the problem of determining the appropriate level of public services.[11] The more public preferences vary geographically, the greater the degree of fragmentation required for allocative efficiency. Fragmentation allows households and businesses to choose between various combinations of taxes and spending.

Even if public preferences are geographically homogeneous, fragmentation is required to ensure technical efficiency in service provision. In order to attract and retain mobile residents and businesses each small unit of local government must ensure value for money, otherwise their customers will 'vote with their feet'. This 'horizontal' fragmentation of the structure of local government provides citizens with information concerning taxes and services in neighbouring areas, thereby raising the competitive pressures on decision makers.

A competitive structure not only implies horizontal fragmentation (a large number of local units) but also vertical fragmentation (several tiers of local government). This has received less attention than horizontal competition in public choice theory.[12] If one authority is responsible for providing all services it can engage in 'full-line forcing', which means that consumers pay one fee for a whole package of services, regardless of their relative valuation of the parts of the package. However, if services are divided between several tiers of local government then their relative costs become visible, and consumers can make separate judgements on the performance of each tier and allocate their political support and tax payments accordingly. Vertical fragmentation within an area forces local authorities to compete for a share of the finite local tax base. This does not mean that there should be one unit for each function, but as many units as are appropriate when the costs of public participation and monitoring are taken into account.[13]

(b) Concentration

The arguments outlined above assume that fragmented institutional arrangements will lead to competitive behaviour and superior performance. However, this conclusion does not follow if a large unit dominates many smaller rivals. In this case, even a fragmented structure may lead to monopolistic behaviour. For this reason, public choice theory emphasises not only fragmentation in the local market, but also the level of concentration.[14] In other words, it is important to consider not only the number of units, but also the distribution of power between them. This dimension of market structure can also be measured horizontally and vertically. Horizontal concentration refers to the distribution of market shares within a tier of local governments, and vertical concentration relates to the shares of different tiers that cover the same area.

In vertically concentrated structures, 'economies of scope' may confer advantages from the provision of a range of services by the same organisation.[15] However, public choice theory cautions that any benefits from economies of scope may be counteracted by low levels of public scrutiny. If many services are provided by a single organisation then it is harder to discern the connection between tax costs and the benefits of any specific service. Moreover, if market share is concentrated in a geographically large top tier, any tendency towards high spending and low efficiency is reinforced by a loss of competitive pressures from fiscal migration.[16] The threat of fiscal migration is greater if market shares are evenly distributed or concentrated in lower-tier units, because the average distance firms or individuals have to move in order to alter their tax and spending packages dramatically is low. By contrast, if market shares are heavily concentrated in large top-tier units then the average relocation distance needed to make a marked difference to the tax and spending ratio is much greater.

Horizontal concentration may also reduce political pressures towards high performance because local authorities with a large market share are in a similar position to large firms: potential dominators of their smaller rivals and beyond the influence of their customers. In contrast, evenly spread market shares mean that local authorities find it more difficult to exploit their neighbours or customers. According to public choice theory, therefore, performance may be higher where market shares are equally distributed.[17]

(c) Flexibility

In addition to fragmentation and deconcentration, a fully competitive local government structure would contain the flexibility to switch services between existing units, and the potential to establish new units or abolish old units. If consumers are unhappy with a service provided by a local authority then they should have the option to transfer the responsibility to another unit. This form of 'consumer power' would pose a permanent competitive threat to existing providers' share of the local government market. Such flexibility is present in the 'Lakewood Plan' established in the USA in the late 1950s. Under this arrangement, municipalities in the Los Angeles area provide services themselves or negotiate contracts with the county. The Lakewood Plan can be regarded as a prototype 'quasi-market' in which public and private producers compete for the custom of local governments.[18]

Citizens should also have the option to establish a new unit to provide a service, such as the special districts for particular services in the USA,[19] and the power to terminate the life of existing units, for example by voluntary merger with a neighbouring municipality. In other words, there should be no barriers to entry or exit in the local government market. The capacity to transfer services and effect structural change allows 'communities of interest' to be defined at different spatial scales, depending on the services to be provided. For example, the geographical size of the relevant community for transport planning is likely to be much bigger than that for the maintenance of local pathways. Also, where services are produced 'in house' a size of unit may be created that minimises costs in relation to circumstances in the local area.

Thus a flexible local government structure would pose a permanent competitive threat to the market share of existing units. A flexible structure implies that business may be lost not only to other areas, but also to other tiers in the same area and to new units entering the market. At the extreme, poor performance by a local unit may result in its disappearance from the local government map.

CRITICISMS OF PUBLIC CHOICE THEORY

While public choice theory has been applied widely in the literature on public policy and local government in the USA, the same can hardly be said about the UK where the approach is viewed at best with scepticism. Four main criticisms of public choice arguments can be identified: the assumptions are unrealistic; the theory has not been tested empirically; even when it has been tested, it is not supported; and even if it is supported, the practical implications are inequitable. The relevance of these criticisms to the public choice model of local government structure will now be considered.

(a) Unrealistic Assumptions?

Public choice models are based on an assumption that human behaviour is primarily selfish rather than altruistic. As Gwartney and Wagner note:

> economists have used the self-interest postulate to develop theories which enhance our understanding of how markets work. Public choice represents an extension of this postulate to politics ... Since there is no evidence that entrance into a voting booth or participation in the political process causes a personality transformation, there is sound reason to believe that the motivation of participants in the market and political process is similar.[20]

This view has been condemned as 'out of touch with reality'[21] and, more strongly, as a 'terrible caricature of reality'.[22]

The standard public choice response to such criticisms is that the realism of the assumptions is irrelevant: all that counts is whether the theoretical models yield predictions which are supported empirically. For example, Downs states that 'theoretical models should be tested primarily by the accuracy of their predictions rather than by the reality of their assumptions'.[23] Similarly, Niskanen argues that 'assumptions should be based only on their usefulness: are [the] assumptions necessary to generate the behavioural hypotheses? Are the behavioural hypotheses confirmed by the available evidence? ... assumptions should specifically not be evaluated by their "realism"'.[24] This does rather beg the question of how a false premise can lead to a true conclusion.[25] Equally, it is illogical to infer that because a model is supported empirically its assumptions must be valid. Nevertheless, if public choice theory is to be evaluated on its own terms, then the focus must shift from assumptions to evidence.

(b) Absence of Evidence?

It has been argued that the public choice literature consists largely of abstract theoretical models which have not been (and perhaps cannot be) tested empirically. For example, Green and Shapiro claim that 'proponents of rational choice seem to be most interested in theory elaboration, leaving for later, or others, the messy business of empirical testing', and 'rational choice scholarship has yet to get off the ground as a rigorous empirical exercise'.[26] Similarly, Dunleavy states that public choice researchers

> often display a thrust towards premature formalization. Major theoretical works emerge, and spawn an increasingly technical literature in which some of the key works' starting assumptions are progressively lost to view. Questions about inherently messy empirical applications are pushed aside by the pace of the development of formal models.[27]

Such criticisms may be valid for some sub-fields of public choice. For example, it is true that many of the articles on the median voter model or bureaucratic power which appear in journals such as the *American Political Science Review* are highly abstract. However, the public choice literature on local government seldom takes this form. The arguments tend to consist of fairly simple verbal propositions rather than complex mathematical formulae. Moreover, there is no shortage of empirical tests of public choice theory on US local government. For example, there is a long tradition of tests of the median voter model,[28] and the impact of bureaucratic power on policy outputs has also been analysed widely.[29] In addition, there have been numerous empirical applications of public choice models of local government structure.[30]

(c) Evidence of Absence?

A third line of attack on public choice theory concedes that empirical tests have been conducted but concludes that the evidence is inconsistent with the theory. For example, Lewin analyses a range of evidence on the behaviour of voters, politicians and bureaucrats.[31] His aim is to investigate whether political actors 'have been influenced not only by their view of what is best for themselves but also what they believe to be best for others, for the community as a whole'.[32] His interpretation of the evidence is that the electorate does not vote 'according to their pocket-books, but rather for the alternative they believe to be best for the country';[33] that 'the image of the politician who is primarily a vote-maximizer has little empirical support';[34] and that 'bureaucrats neither may, can, dare, nor want to maximise the budget in the manner Niskanen assumed they would'.[35]

Lewin's interpretation of the evidence on public choice theory is, however, both partial and skewed. It is partial because it ignores most of the empirical studies on US local government noted in section (b) above; and skewed because the evidence in many of these studies is consistent with public choice hypotheses on voting behaviour, party competition and bureaucratic power. For example, the 'house journal' of the public choice movement, *Public Choice,* is replete with results which are consistent with the self-interest axiom. Lewin (and perhaps the political science community more generally) seems unaware of such studies. This is not to argue that his conclusion should be turned on its head, but simply to point out that the empirical validity of public choice theory remains an open question.

Although most empirical analyses of public choice theory and local government have been undertaken in the USA, there is a small quantity of evidence in the UK.[36] A recent example is the study by John, Dowding and Biggs, who test the relationship between household movements and local taxes and services in four London boroughs. They find that, in a sample of 860 households which had moved during the period of the poll tax, almost half cited taxes or services as important influences on their decision to reside in a particular location. Moreover, residential choices were 'Tiebout-rational': households which emphasised the importance of taxes moved to low-tax boroughs, while those which stressed service levels moved to boroughs with a reputation for better services. John *et al.* conclude that their results 'demonstrate to a sceptical British urban studies community that public choice is not to be lightly dismissed with a critique of its unrealistic assumptions'.[37]

(d) Inequitable Outcomes?

In the private sector, market processes lead to a distribution of resources that reflects the criterion of 'ability to pay'. An important criticism of public choice theory is that the introduction of competition into the public sector produces the same result: high-income groups receive a disproportionate share of public services. This outcome is inconsistent with a definition of equity which requires that resources are allocated according to need rather than ability to pay. The concepts of equity and justice have been given scant attention by public choice theorists.[38] The main emphasis has been on performance criteria such as responsiveness and efficiency, but these are not politically neutral terms. In order to judge responsiveness, it is necessary to know whose preferences are being met. Also, the same level of technical efficiency (the ratio of inputs to outputs) may be obtained at high and low levels of service provision. In this case there is no single optimum scale of production which follows 'logically' from the criterion of efficiency.

To what extent, then, is the public choice model of local government structure inherently inequitable? Are the needs of low-income groups inevitably neglected in a competitive structure? The major criticisms have been directed at horizontal fragmentation which, it is claimed, stratifies localities into rich and poor areas.[39] Also, if the threat of fiscal migration forces councils to compete for wealthy households, then policies will favour this section of the community, and redistribution to the poor will be prevented. Peterson argues that in the USA

> policies vary depending on the structure of local government systems. In big cities, where local governments are large and have monopoly control over a large land area, some degree of redistribution occurs even at the local level. Where local governments are small, numerous, and highly competitive with one another, as in suburbia, redistribution is kept to a minimum.[40]

However, it is important to note that evidence in the UK suggests that large, centralised welfare bureaucracies deliver services which are *formally* redistributive but *effectively* favour the middle class.[41] Thus a high quantity of 'redistributive' services should not be confused with equity. Furthermore, it has been argued that redistribution is more effectively and efficiently pursued by central than by local government.[42] In this case, redistribution can be pursued independently of local structural arrangements. Finally, even if horizontal fragmentation is associated with inequity, it is not clear that the other elements of the public choice model are culpable on this count. Why should councils in vertically fragmented, deconcentrated and flexible local government structures discriminate against low-income groups? Neither public choice theorists nor their critics have addressed these issues. It is therefore inappropriate to conclude that public choice principles automatically lead to inequitable outcomes in local government.

(e) Summary

The major criticisms of public choice theory have limited application to the model of local government structure outlined in this paper. First, the assumptions of the model may be unrealistic, but public choice theorists would argue that this is unimportant: if empirical evidence is consistent with the model then the assumptions 'work'. Moreover, if political behaviour is motivated more strongly by selfishness than selflessness, public choice models are likely to meet with some empirical success. Secondly, a substantial number of tests of public choice theory have been conducted – it is not simply an abstract intellectual pursuit with no empirical applications. Thirdly, the empirical tests provide evidence both for and against public choice theory, so it is premature to dismiss its practical validity. And, finally, there is little evidence to suggest that the structural arrangements favoured by public choice theory are more inequitable than alternative arrangements.

None of these points are intended to demonstrate that the public choice model is empirically valid or normatively desirable. Rather, a balanced conclusion is that the model is worthy of further investigation. It is to this task that the discussion now turns.

REORGANISATION IN SCOTLAND AND WALES

The main elements of reorganisation in Scotland and Wales are fairly simple. In Scotland, the nine regions and 53 districts established in 1975 have been replaced by 29 unitary authorities. The three island councils, hitherto anomalies in a two-tier system, retain their unitary status. In Wales, the eight counties and 37 districts created in 1974 have been replaced by a new structure comprising 22 units. The process of reorganisation in both countries was similar: the government stated an initial preference for a single-tier system; carried out a 'consultation' exercise which largely involved individual councils, local government associations and professional bodies; then ignored the results of consultation by implementing its initial plan, albeit with some marginal changes.[43] A common arithmetic formula for reorganisation also seems to have been used in Scotland and Wales: add up the number of upper-tier and lower-tier councils, divide by two, and round down to the nearest politically acceptable figure. To what extent do the outcomes reflect public choice principles?

In order to assess changes in structure it is necessary to identify the organisations that count as part of the local government system.[44] Two types of local authorities can be distinguished: primary units which are directly elected and have tax raising powers, and secondary units which possess only one of these characteristics.[45] Following this framework, measures of structure should take both primary and secondary units into account; and organisations which are neither directly elected nor possess tax powers can be excluded from the analysis.

(a) Fragmentation

According to public choice theory there should be as much vertical fragmentation as necessary to balance the marginal benefits of inter-tier competition with the marginal costs of democratic control. This seems to require at least two tiers of local governments, but the exact number in an ideal public choice structure is unclear. A pure unitary system is directly at odds with public choice principles because there would be no vertical fragmentation: all functions would be consolidated in a single tier of primary councils. This is not, however, the outcome in Scotland and Wales. In addition to the tier of primary units, there are several tiers of secondary units. First, some bodies with tax precepting powers operate above the scale of the unitary authorities. For example, separate joint boards have responsibility for services such as fire and police. In addition, the government has reserve powers to establish joint bodies for the provision of other services if it deems that the unitary authorities are not performing to a satisfactory standard. There is also a tier of secondary local government below the unitary authorities in some areas. This tier consists of 'area committees' which may take responsibility for almost all former district and county/regional services. Area committees have no tax raising powers but are directly elected (councillors are elected simultaneously to the unitary authority and the area committee). The pressure to establish such committees was strongest in districts which sought but did not achieve unitary status. In Wales, for example, each of the former districts within the new Gwynedd unitary authority is represented by an area committee with powers over services including housing, social services and education.

Thus vertical fragmentation persists in the new structure: while the fragmentation of primary local government has declined to its lowest possible point, the fragmentation of secondary local government has increased. The question for public choice theory is whether the extra secondary tiers can provide competitive pressures which compensate for the loss of rivalry between the two former primary tiers. The public choice literature provides neither theory nor evidence that sheds light on this issue. However, given the emphasis on public accountability in much public choice writing, it is likely that one tier of primary units would be valued more highly than several tiers of secondary units.

There are also some difficulties in identifying an ideal pattern of horizontal fragmentation in the public choice model. There should be a sufficiently large number of units to provide households and businesses with genuine locational choices in the local government market, but how many units in each tier does this imply? At the extreme, each neighbourhood or street might form a separate local unit, but this would hardly be 'government' in any meaningful sense. Nevertheless it is worth recalling that a little over 20 years ago there were local governments in Scotland and Wales with as few as 300 and 500 residents respectively.[46] Proponents of public choice theory could no doubt find arguments to defend this degree of horizontal fragmentation, at least for the lowest tier of councils.

While it is difficult to use public choice theory to prescribe an optimum number of local units, an interpretation of the *change* in horizontal fragmentation in 1996 is more straightforward. As a result of reorganisation, the number of local authorities providing former district services has declined by more than half, while roughly three times as many units are now providing former county/regional services. The upper-tier councils were responsible for the major local government functions and around 85 per cent of expenditure funded by grants and local taxes. Thus the net outcome of reorganisation is that local services are more horizontally fragmentated. From a public choice perspective, there is more potential for competitive pressures towards responsiveness and efficiency, for example as a result of fiscal migration.

(b) Concentration

Public choice arguments on concentration imply that an equal distribution of market shares across tiers or between the units within a tier will stimulate good performance. By contrast, if a part of the local government system has a high market share then this is likely to impair efficiency and responsiveness.

TABLE I

HORIZONTAL CONCENTRATION (DISTRIBUTION OF POPULATION ACROSS LOCAL UNITS)

	Mean	CV[1]	Minimum Population[2]		Maximum Population	
WALES						
Counties	359	0.34	117	(Powys)	535	(Mid Glamorgan)
Districts	78	0.61	23	(Radnor)	285	(Cardiff)
New Councils	131	0.40	67	(Cardiganshire)	295	(Cardiff)
SCOTLAND						
Regions	559	1.15	104	(Borders)	2,306	(Strathclyde)
Districts	95	1.13	10	(Nairn)	689	(Glasgow)
New Councils	174	0.72	49	(Clackmannan)	624	(Glasgow)

Notes:
1. Coefficient of variation
2. Population in thousands

Horizontal concentration can be measured by analysing the distribution of population across local units in a given geographical market.[47] The variation in population across units in the old and new local government systems is shown in Table 1. In Scotland, market shares are more evenly spread in the new structure than in the old: the coefficient of variation for population size is substantially lower in the unitary authorities than in the regions and districts. This is partly because of the removal from the local government map of units at the extremes of the population range (for example, Strathclyde region and Nairn district). Big urban authorities such as Glasgow and Edinburgh retain a dominant position in their territorial sub-markets, but from a public choice perspective the greater equalisation of market shares is a positive outcome. In Wales, the impact of reorganisation on horizontal concentration is more mixed. The population sizes of the new units are spread more evenly than the former districts, but more widely than the counties. The net effect of structural change on the geographical distribution of power in the local government market is therefore indeterminate.

Population figures cannot be used to assess vertical concentration because several tiers cover the same territory. This dimension of vertical structure can be measured with financial data, such as the share of total local government spending taken by each tier. It is not possible as yet to apply this measure because expenditure out-turn data for the new unitary, supra-unitary and sub-unitary authorities are not available. Nevertheless, it is possible to conclude that the new pattern of vertical concentration will be an improvement from a public choice perspective. The unitary authorities seem likely to retain, on average, the highly dominant market share of the regions and counties. However, there is less potential for monopolistic behaviour because the new councils are subject to greater pressures from horizontal competition than were the former upper-tier authorities.

(c) Flexibility

Local government reorganisation in Scotland and Wales has bestowed no new powers on the public to alter structural arrangements. Indeed, the very process of reform lacked sensitivity to geographical variations in public preferences. The English commission seemed to attach great weight to public opinion polls, and largely adopted the most popular (or least unpopular) option in each area. This resulted in the retention of the two-tier *status quo* in most areas, and the creation of unitary authorities in only a minority of cases. It seems likely that a similar diversity of structures would have emerged in Scotland and Wales if a similar process of public consultation had been followed.

Thus the new local government system is no more flexible than the old. Local communities cannot secede from their unitary authority; nor do they have the discretion to form a new larger unit of primary local government by voluntary merger with a unitary neighbour. Indeed, in Wales at least, reorganisation has been accompanied by less flexibility. Under the 1974 Local Government Act, local electors could vote by a simple referendum to abolish their community council (the third tier of primary units, below the counties and the districts). After the introduction of the poll tax in 1990, community councils became responsible for meeting all of their own costs. The result was considerable public disquiet at the apparently high poll taxes levied by some community councils in exchange for only minor services. Attempts were made to remove a number of these units through referenda, and two were abolished by this mechanism (Vaynor in Mid Glamorgan, and Rhoose in South Glamorgan). This flexibility 'loophole' in the legislation has been closed in the new local government system.

CONCLUSION

Public choice theory suggests that local government systems perform best when there is vertical and horizontal fragmentation, and when market shares are evenly spread rather than concentrated in a single tier or in a few large units within a tier. In addition, all units should be under the competitive threat that the public will seek to transfer responsibility for a service to another unit, establish an entirely new unit, or abolish an existing unit.

This model leads to a number of conclusions concerning local government reorganisation in Scotland and Wales. Some dimensions of structure have been changed for the better from a public choice perspective. First, there is more horizontal fragmentation because the number of units responsible for providing the major local government services has increased. Secondly, the new pattern of vertical concentration is better than the old because the dominant market share is held by a tier with a larger number of units. And, thirdly, horizontal concentration has improved in Scotland, although there is little change in Wales. However, vertical fragmentation has moved away from the public choice model in the new structure because a tier of primary local government has been lost; and there is no flexibility in the new structure because there are complete barriers to entry and exit in the local government market.

The public choice verdict on reorganisation therefore depends on whether the deterioration in vertical fragmentation is outweighed by the improvements in horizontal fragmentation and in vertical and horizontal concentration. The problem is that the relative importance of the various dimensions of structure has not been addressed in the public choice literature. Thus public choice theory permits no definite judgement on the relative merits of the old and new structures. In addition, as noted above, the theoretical framework is not sufficiently detailed to generate clear prescriptions on an ideal local government structure. Questions such as 'how many tiers should there be?' and 'what is the optimum number of units in each tier' find no precise answers in public choice theory. Despite the aura of economic logic which surrounds public choice theory, it does not deliver a 'rational plan' for local government structure from first principles. The reason may be that it is not truly a deductive theory; rather it is derived inductively from the characteristics of local government in the USA. Therefore, when an attempt is made to apply the public choice model of local government structure it leads to loose ends rather than tight conclusions.

NOTES

1. E. Ostrom, 'Metropolitan Reform: Propositions Derived from Two Traditions', *Social Science Quarterly*, 53 (1972), pp.474–93.
2. L.J. Sharpe, 'Local Government Reorganization: General Theory and U.K. Practice', in B. Dente and F. Kjellberg (eds.), *The Dynamics of Institutional Change* (London: Sage, 1988), p.121.
3. G.A. Boyne, 'Local Government: From Monopoly to Competition?', in G. Jordan and N. Ashford (eds.), *Public Policy and the Impact of the New Right* (London: Pinter, 1993).
4. For an account of the politics of reoganisation see G. Boyne, G. Jordan and M. McVicar, *Local Government Reform: A Review of the Process in Scotland and Wales* (York: Joseph Rowntree Foundation, 1995).
5. E. Ostrom and V. Ostrom, 'A Behavioural Approach to the Study of Intergovernmental Relations', *Annals of the American Academy of Political and Social Science* 359 (1965), pp.137–46; M. Schneider, *The Competitive City* (Pittsburgh: University of Pittsburgh Press, 1989).
6. G.A. Boyne, 'Competition and Local Government: A Public Choice Perspective', *Urban Studies*, 33 (1996), pp.703–21.
7. V. Ostrom, *The Intellectual Crisis in American Public Administration* (Tuscaloosa: University of Alabama Press, 1989).
8. A. Breton and A. Scott, *The Economic Constitution of Federal States* (Toronto: University of Toronto Press, 1978).
9. G.A. Boyne, 'Population Size and Economies of Scale in Local Government', *Policy and Politics*, 23 (1995), pp.213–22.
10. R. Bish and R. Warren, 'Scale and Monopoly Problems in Urban Public Services', *Urban Affairs Quarterly*, 8 (1975), pp.97–122.
11. C. Tiebout, 'A Pure Theory of Local Expenditure', *Journal of Political Economy*, 64 (1956), pp.416–42.
12. G. Belanger, 'Federalism and Local Government', *European Journal of Political Economy*, 3 (1987), pp.131–49; C. Wagoner, 'Local Fiscal Competition: An Intraregional Perspective', *Public Finance Quarterly*, 23 (1995), pp.95–114.
13. Bish and Warren, 'Scale and Monopoly Problems in Urban Public Services'.
14. E. Ostrom, 'A Public Service Industry Approach to the Study of Local Government Structure and Performance', *Policy and Politics*, 11 (1983), pp.313–41.
15. S. Grosskopf and Y. Yaisawarng, 'Economies of Scope in the Provision of Local Public Services', *National Tax Journal*, 43 (1990), pp.61–74.
16. P. Grossman, 'Fiscal Decentralization and Government Size', *Public Choice*, 62 (1989), pp.63–9; J. Zax, 'Is There A Leviathan In Your Neighbourhood?', *American Economic Review*, 79 (1989), pp.560–67.
17. R. Eberts and T. Gronberg, 'Structure, Conduct and Performance in the Local Public Sector', *National Tax Journal*, 43 (1990), pp.165–73.
18. R. Warren, *Government in Metropolitan Areas: A Reappraisal of Fractionated Political Organization* (University of California, Institute of Governmental Affairs, 1966).

19. V. Ostrom, R. Bish and E. Ostrom, *Local Government in the United States* (San Francisco: Institute For Contemporary Studies Press, 1988).
20. J. Gwartney and R. Wagner, 'Public Choice and the Conduct of Representative Government', in Gwartney and Wagner (eds.), *Public Choice and Constitutional Economics* (London: JAI Press, 1988), p.7.
21. T. Degregori, 'Caveat Emptor: A Critique of the Emerging Paradigm of Public Choice', *Administration and Society*, 6 (1974), p.205.
22. S. Kelman, 'Public Choice and Public Spirit', *Public Interest*, 87 (1987), p.81. For a rejoinder see G. Brennan and J. Buchanan, 'Is Public Choice Immoral: The Case for the "Nobel" Lie', *Virginia Law Review*, 74 (1988), pp.179–89.
23. A. Downs, *An Economic Theory of Democracy* (New York: Harper and Row, 1957), p.21.
24. W. Niskanen, *Bureaucracy and Representative Government* (Chicago: Aldine-Atherton, 1971), p.10.
25. J. Toye, 'Economic Theories of Politics and Public Finance', *British Journal of Political Science*, 6 (1976), pp.433–47.
26. P. Green and I. Shapiro, *Pathologies of Rational Choice Theory* (New Haven: Yale University Press, 1994), p.7.
27. P. Dunleavy, *Democracy, Bureaucracy and Public Choice* (London: Harvester Wheatsheaf, 1991), p.xi.
28. J. Barr and O. Davies, 'An Elementary Political and Economic Theory of The Expenditures of Local Governments', *Southern Economic Journal*, 33 (1966), pp.149–65; G. Turnbull and S. Djoundourian, 'The Median Voter Hypothesis: Evidence from General Purpose Local Governments', *Public Choice*, 81 (1994), pp.223–40.
29. M. Ott, 'Bureaucracy, Monopoly and the Demand for Municipal Services', *Journal of Urban Economics*, 8 (1980), pp.362–82; S. Mehay and R. Gonzalez, 'Outside Information and the Monopoly Power of a Public Bureau: An Empirical Analysis', *Public Finance Quarterly*, 15 (1987), pp.61–75.
30. For example, tests of the Tiebout hypothesis are reviewed by K. Dowding, P. John and J. Biggs, 'Tiebout: A Survey of The Empirical Literature', *Urban Studies*, 31 (1994), pp.769–97; and evidence on the impact of structure on spending is summarised in G.A. Boyne, 'Local Government Structure and Performance: Lessons from America?', *Public Administration*, 70 (1992), pp.333–57.
31. L. Lewin, *Self Interest and Public Interest in Western Politics* (Oxford: Oxford University Press, 1991); see also L. Udehn, *The Limits of Public Choice* (London: Routledge, 1996).
32. Lewin, *Self Interest and Public Interest in Western Politics*, p.25.
33. Ibid., p.45.
34. Ibid., p.74.
35. Ibid., p.89.
36. G.A. Boyne, *Constraints, Choices and Public Policies* (London: JAI Press, 1996), Ch.6.
37. P. John, K. Dowding and J. Biggs 'Residential Mobility in London: A Micro-Level Test of the Behavioural Assumptions of the Tiebout Model', *British Journal of Political Science*, 25 (1995), p.396.
38. K. Dowding 'Public Choice and Local Governance', in D. King and G. Stoker (eds.), *Rethinking Local Democracy* (London: Macmillan, 1996); S. Kolm, 'Moral Public Choice', *Public Choice*, 87 (1996), pp.117–41.
39. K. Newton, 'American Urban Politics: Social Class, Political Structure and Public Goods', *Urban Affairs Quarterly*, 11 (1975), pp.241–64; E. Ostrom, 'The Social Stratification–Government Inequality Thesis Re-examined', *Urban Affairs Quarterly*, 19 (1983), pp.91–112.
40. P. Peterson, *City Limits* (Chicago: University of Chicago Press, 1981), p.16.
41. J. Le Grand, *The Strategy of Equality* (London: George Allen and Unwin, 1982).
42. H. Ladd and F. Doolittle, 'Which Level of Government should Assist the Poor', *National Tax Journal*, 35 (1982), pp.323–36; C. Brown and W. Oates, 'Assistance to the Poor in a Federal System', *Journal of Public Economics*, 32 (1987), pp.307–30.
43. G.A. Boyne and J. Law, 'Bidding for Unitary Status: An Evaluation of the Contest in Wales', *Local Government Studies*, 19 (1993), pp.537–57.

44. M. Cole and G.A. Boyne, 'So You Think You Know What Local Government Is', *Local Government Studies*, 21 (1995), pp.191–205.
45. J. Stanyer, *Understanding Local Government* (Oxford: Martin Robertson, 1980).
46. Boyne *et al.*, *Local Government Reform: A Review of the Process in Scotland and Wales*.
47. G.A. Boyne and M. Cole, 'Fragmentation, Concentration and Local Government Structure: Top-Tier Authorities in England and Wales, 1831–1996', *Government and Policy*, 14 (1996), pp.501–14.

Local Government Reform in Scotland: Managing the Transition

ARTHUR MIDWINTER AND NEIL McGARVEY

Scotland's new unitary local councils have now been in existence for over a year. The transition from a two-tier structure of nine regions and 53 districts to 29 unitary authorities on the Scottish mainland is now largely complete. The following seeks to review the reorganisation process. It first reviews the government arguments which underpinned the case for change. The focus then turns to how the reorganisation has been managed and reviews the impact of tightening finances and new managerial ideas. Finally, emerging issues such as what we have termed 'patronage politics' as well as devolution are reviewed.

An important point to stress about the reorganisation in Scotland, as opposed to that in England, is the top-down nature of its imposition. There was no equivalent of the Local Government Commission. It was largely implemented in a non-consensual, highly partisan environment. This despite the fact that all opposition parties in Scotland had in recent years adopted policies favouring reorganisation.[1] During the reorganisation process the Convention of Scottish Local Authorities (COSLA) actively pursued a non-cooperation strategy, indicative of the highly political atmosphere which surrounded the process.

The roots of the reorganisation can be traced to Mrs Thatcher's fall from power in 1990. After this the government committed itself to a review of the structure, finance and management of local government. The government's case for a single-tier structure was presented in the first of its consultation papers.[2] This argued that the Wheatley two-tier system established in 1974 was not readily understood, that this clouded accountability, and that large authorities were remote, bureaucratic and inefficient. The second consultation paper[3] argued for authorities based on local allegiances, and put forward four options on the number of authorities (15, 24, 35 and 51). The end product was a system of 32 authorities, which would clarify accountability and reduce administrative costs established through the Local Government (Scotland) Act 1994.

Arthur Midwinter and Neil McGarvey, University of Strathclyde

REORGANISATION: RATIONALE AND CRITIQUE

The government's stated objectives were to improve efficiency and enhance democracy. These objectives represent the twin poles between democracy and efficiency which face all would-be reformers of local government. The Scottish Secretary held the view that dismantling the large regional authorities would lead to a simpler and more efficient structure. The government did not go so far in either rhetoric or substance with the reforms as the Conservative Right would have wished, neither reducing the scope of local government nor adopting the very small units that the Right wished.[4] Concern over costs and savings 'proved important in weighting ministerial views against too localist a solution'.[5]

In promoting the two explicit objectives, the government's proposals were based on a number of key assumptions. Firstly, it was assumed that community loyalties remained with the pre-1974 local authorities. A return to community-based local government would revitalise local government, increase public interest and hence electoral turnout. Secondly, it assumed that the use of joint arrangements would be consistent with promoting accountability:

> This need not however mean that an individual authority would relinquish control or responsibility for the provision of a service. The government are determined that an important aspect of the new single-tier local authorities should be clear lines of accountability between local people and those they have elected to represent them. There is nothing new in local authorities combining to provide services: various arrangements already exist in the current system ranging from joint boards for police and fire to the use by smaller authorities of specialist facilities which are provided only by the larger authorities.[6]

Thirdly, the government assumed that the development of the enabling role of authorities meant that large authorities providing economies of scale were no longer necessary. To quote again from 'Shaping the New Councils', the government claimed there is now:

> a general recognition that many services are better delivered by competing private business. They [local authorities] now buy a wide range of services from the private sector, so that there is less need for them to maintain a comprehensive range of expertise within their own organisation. Taken together these factors reduce the need for very large authorities of the sort Wheatley recommended.[7]

The notions that there were problems of confusion and community identification caused by the two-tier system were not confined to the government. The Labour Party, arguing for reform in the context of Scottish devolution, felt that the two-tier system was confusing and less accountable than a system of unitary authorities.[8] However, a number of research studies have shown, community identity operates mainly at a level *lower* than local government units. The research for Wheatley showed that primary loyalties were to the neighbourhood. There was in fact little identification with the former counties, and it is difficulty to see such identification being meaningful to those new voters since 1975.[9] Research carried out for the Widdicombe Committee showed much greater levels of understanding of the two-tier system than the conventional wisdom suggests.[10] A similar picture holds in England, where Bristow argued there was strong evidence that the primary identification is directed towards the neighbourhood rather than town or county, confirmed in a recent MORI study.[11] As one former Local Government Commissioner put it, there are problems with:

> the idea that the map of communities may translate into a map of local authorities. The idea is clearly valid in the case of big cities such as Derby and Southampton. Elsewhere, through, as the Commission discovered from the MORI surveys it commissioned and summarised in the report setting out its draft recommendations for review areas, the general majority of people identify most strongly with geographical areas which are smaller than most existing districts – the parish or small town. It was wishful thinking to suppose that a self-evident pattern of 'natural communities' exists at a geographical scale that could provide the general basis for local government units which would wield all the powers of existing counties and districts and simultaneously secure effective and convenient local government.[12]

It is clear that the conventional orthodoxy that small local authorities will be more responsive and more democratic retains a hold in the minds of politicians. It is also clear that small scale is usually associated with fewer functions.[13] In Scotland, the creation of smaller units was indeed achieved through a loss of functions such as trunk roads, water and sewerage, the reporter's administration, and the need for extended use of joint arrangements for service provision. Three-quarters of the new authorities are smaller than 200,000 population (see Table 1).

As well as the stated objectives outlined, there is little doubt that local government reorganisation was driven by political considerations. Boyne, Jordan and McVicar[14] referred to the desire of the Conservatives to transfer power to Tory constituencies, such as Bearsden, Eastwood and Stirling, where the party held 'legitimate political interests'. Black[15] identifies Stirling, Perth and Kinross, Kyle and Carrick and Eastwood as being Tory districts which survived as a result of party political considerations. In addition, ward-level adjustments were made in Dundee to enhance the prospect of Tory control in Angus. Structural decisions were thus compromised by the need to accommodate the Conservative's partisan objectives, which led to some ten authorities with populations of less than 100,000.

The new map of local government in Scotland is based on seven former regional/islands authority areas, 12 former district authority areas, and 13 as amalgamations of former districts of parts of them. This, as indicated earlier, pays no attention to the pattern of community loyalties which lie below such units. The anticipated community identification with the new authorities is therefore suspect. Indeed, actual turnout actually fell by two per cent in the first elections to the new authorities compared with an average of 40 per cent since 1974, and again in the most recent regional election of 1994. The reorganisation has also seen the growth of secondary local government at the expense of primary local government which 'consists of local authorities who have stable and clearly marked boundaries, are responsible for a range of public services, and have an independent power of local taxation, in addition to having their members directly elected'.[16] The number of primary units was decreased from 65 to 32, whilst the number of secondary units was increased from seven to 32, comprising 23 joint boards, four joint committees and five new quangos (see Table 1).

TABLE 1
SECONDARY LOCAL GOVERNMENT IN SCOTLAND 1997

Joint Boards

Six Joint Police Boards
Six Joint Fire Boards
Ten Valuation Joint Boards
The Strathclyde Passenger Transport Authority

Joint Committees

Strathclyde Central Purchasing
Tayside Contracts
North East Scotland Library Services
Scottish Local Government Information Unit

Non-Departmental Public Bodies

Three Water Authorities
The Scottish Children's Reporters Administration
The Scottish Environmental Protection Agency

Most researchers see joint boards as weakening democracy[17] and breaking the clear lines of accountability sought by the government. The best analysis of this is that of Leach, Davies, Game and Skelcher, who concluded:

> joint action for anything other than a very limited range of services should be seen as additional (indirectly elected) tier of local government which actually undermines, in a fundamental sense, the 'unitary authority' principle. It raises major issues about processes of resource allocation, public comprehensibility and in particular, public accountability.[18]

The reality is of a further fragmentation of political responsibility caused by the desiderata of small authorities.

Another central assumption of the government's agenda was that financial savings would arise from reorganisation, mainly in central administration and concurrent services, with the quality and quantity of front-line services remaining unchanged. The estimated savings were derived from financial modelling techniques.[19] The realism of the modelling has been extensively challenged;[20] weaknesses were acknowledged by the Scottish Office and the scale of net savings scaled down to £40 million per annum, with an expected manpower reduction of 300–1,800 resulting from the reforms. The next two sections will review developments in the fields of both staffing and finance in order that a preliminary assessment of the government's efficiency assumptions can be made.

MANAGING THE TRANSITION

(i) Finance

Overall, only minimal transitional costs were assumed by the government. The prospects for a smooth transition to the new authorities was dimmed however, by an extremely tight financial settlement for 1996–97, resulting from a tough public expenditure round. This meant that the new authorities faced three potential sources of income loss.

Firstly, the government made provision for £30 millions of savings accruing from reorganisation. This was based on the assumption that central support services and district services will be cheaper to manage because of the reduction in the number of authorities, and administration of regional services will be more expensive as their units would increase. Greatest savings were therefore expected in the aggregating authorities, where district services were being amalgamated on a regional basis, and no new authority for regional services was required. Large savings were also anticipated from urban authorities. Interestingly, *increased* costs of administration were expected in most of the contentious 'gerrymandered' authorities, such as East Renfrewshire, East Dunbartonshire and Stirling.

Secondly, special problems arose in disaggregating regions through what became known as the mismatch problem. Regional budgets were disaggregated into notional budgets for the new authorities, and compared with their prospective Grant Aided Expenditure (GAE) assessments, the Scottish equivalent of Standard Spending Assessments. Large savings, for example, would be required in Dundee (£9m), Glasgow (£28m), Midlothian (£6m) and Argyll and Bute (£7m), whilst gains would arise in East Renfrewshire (£5m), Angus (£4m) and Aberdeenshire (£14m). Not surprisingly, the full impact of both these factors was 'dampened' by various means, including a last-minute intervention by the Secretary of State.

In addition, there was the general expectation of self-funding pay settlements through efficiency gains in the public sector, which would mean a real cut in grant income of 3–4 per cent for most authorities. The budget situation was also exacerbated by the extensive use of creative accounting techniques during 1995–96 to keep council taxes down in election year. The combined effect of these factors was a serious fiscal problem for local authorities. As the scale of cuts on offer became public, the Scottish Secretary intervened in the week prior to budget fixing to provide a further £100 million aid package through creative accounting, whereby capital allocations could be used to fund revenue spending in the transitional year. Widespread public protest over potential school closures made such political intervention inevitable. Ministers continued to insist that cuts in services/tax increases were unnecessary, and that the efficiency savings provision was realistic.

(ii) Staffing

As well as having financial implications, the reorganisation was also likely to have a significant impact on staff. In order to safeguard the interests of staff in the transition period a Staff Commission was set up with the following remit:

- Considering and keeping under review the arrangements for the recruitment of staff by new local authorities and for the transfer of staff employees by existing authorities which cease to exist;
- considering such staff problems arising as may be referred to it by the Secretary of State or by any authority;
- advising the Secretary of State as to the steps necessary to safeguard the interests of such staff; and
- advising authorities.[21]

The Commission took the view that it wished to see maximum job retention in the new authorities. Its advice on recruitment 'ring-fenced' senior posts initially to candidates from within Scottish local government, unlike England and Wales where there was open competition. Although there was a political campaign of 'non-cooperation' in 1994, staff issues were exempted and consultation and planning proceeded, albeit less comprehensively than if there had been political consensus on the reforms. The Commission stressed the need to transfer operations as going concerns, to maintain continuity of service to the public. Compulsory redundancy was to be a last resort. The Commission estimated that around 90 per cent of staff would simply transfer to authorities where either their establishment or department was taken over in its entirety. A process of matching would be required for staff who did not fit into these categories (that is, the existing workload would be shared between new authorities). They also advocated non-filling of vacancies and use of temporary posts to minimise the need for redundancy. Arrangements were made to facilitate movement between transfer lists in cases of surpluses/shortfalls. Despite these efforts to maintain employment, the financial settlement became problematic. Authorities did take short-term action over freezing vacancies and permitting early retirement to try to avoid redundancies, which were isolated.

The government began with a rosy scenario of limited job loss in central administration and concurrent services. In November 1995 Michael Forsyth, the Secretary of State for Scotland, estimated job losses arising from reorganisation would be a maximum of 1,800. In addition, the government pointed to duplication in terms of planning, industrial development and urban renewal. This should *not* be construed to mean authorities were providing duplicate services. Regions and districts had distinct planning roles, and different approaches to urban renewal. In total, these activities amounted to 2.2 per cent of local expenditure.[22] The scope for savings was never extensive. The assumption seems to be that such losses would have negligible effect on front-line service provision. What was the result in practice?

Table 2 outlines the aggregate change in staffing within Scottish local authorities during the initial transition period. As the table shows, only a matter of a few months after the set up of the new councils there was considerable job reduction, with councils employing 6,700 fewer FTEs. Analysing these figures by service reveals that it is education which has bore the brunt of the job losses. Non-statutory services such as libraries, museums and galleries have also suffered.

TABLE 2
STAFFING IN THE TRANSITIONAL PERIOD

Full Time Eqivalents in Scottish Local Authorities

Year	FTE
December 1994	246,982
September 1995	246,907
September 1996	240,198

Notes: Figures for all years exclude Water, Sewerage & other transferred services not currently within the remit of local authorities.

Source: Scottish Office/COSLA Joint Staffing Watch, January 1997

TABLE 3
STAFFING FIGURES BY SERVICE

	Dec. 94	Sept. 95	Sept. 96
Education – Teaching	53,654	52,507	52,232
Education – Non-Teaching	24,480	24,628	20,884
Libraries, Museums & Galleries	4,569	4,734	4,326
Social Services*	38,587	38,074	38,784
Housing	7,829	7,916	7,955

Note: *Estimate 275 transferred with children's reporter service excluded

Source: Scottish Office/COSLA Joint Staffing Watch, January 1997

Fully comprehensive comparable time series data on the impact of reorganisation on the costs of administration and concurrent services is not yet available. CIPFA's Rating Review does produce data for the costs of corporate management, education and housing management; and for total spending on the former concurrent services of planning and industrial development and leisure and recreation, and these are displayed in Table 4 for indicative purposes. These figures show that there has been a reduction of those involved in direct service delivery, and the total manpower has been adjusted for the reduced scope to local government to exceed the government manpower predictions of a loss of 1,800 posts. The budgetary retrenchment resulted in several authorities freezing posts.

Comparison of the two systems on current prices reveals a very modest increase of £200,000 in the new system over the old system. The cost of corporate management is stable, despite the reduction in the number of chief executives; there is a minor fall in the costs of education administration despite the increase in the number of education authorities; and a rise in the costs of housing management despite the decrease in the number of housing authorities. Similarly, whilst the costs of leisure and recreation have fallen, the costs of planning and industrial development have risen. This, of course, will reflect differing political judgements about the social and organisational needs of the new authorities from their predecessors. In short there is no evidence as yet of savings in administrative and concurrent services resulting from reorganisation.

TABLE 4
COST OF MANAGEMENT AND CONCURRENT SERVICES IN THE OLD AND NEW SYSTEMS

	1994–95	1995–96
	(Old System)	New System)
Corporate Management	£56m	56.5m
Housing Management	£153.2m	£150.7m
Education Management	£70.3m	£74.4m
Planning and Industrial Dept	£71.6m	£60.1m
Leisure and Recreation	£294.6m	£303.8m
TOTAL	£645.7m	£645.5m

Source: CIPFA Rating Review 1994/95 and 1995/96

From the CIPFA Rating Review, we also note that the budgets of local government as a whole rose by around four per cent and the gap between authorities budgets and GAE rose from 3.3 per cent to 6.3 per cent, with 27 of the 32 authorities spending above GAE. This suggests that under a universal (as opposed to selective) capping regime councils were learning to play the system.[23] In April 1996 an average council tax increase of 17 per cent (based on Band D properties) was the result. This was not the pattern sought by government.

What these figures show is that in the context of labour-intensive local service provision, there is really only one way 'efficiency' savings can be achieved: provision of the same level of service with fewer personnel. To assume that all cuts in personnel would occur at the corporate centre and that front-line service delivery would not be affected was quite fanciful on the government's part.

(iii) The New Management Agenda

The remit if the Staff Commission in Scotland did not include advice and guidance on managerial practice. Thus, unlike the Paterson Report in the 1970s there was no managerial blueprint for the new authorities. A Working Group to look into management was established in 1992. This was chaired by the local government minister, with members from the Scottish Office, local government, the Accounts Commission and the Commissioner of Local Administration. Stress was placed on the individual responsibility for management issues of councils themselves, but the group looked at the identification of statutory obstacles to management innovation in councils. Radical reforms, such as directly elected mayors, were rejected. The development of the enabling authority model was seen as offering prospects for flatter management structures, whilst in local government some held a view that this was the opportunity to strengthen corporate control further, and rationalise the committee and departmental structures into cognate services.[24] Overall, in terms of managerial practice the Scottish Office was quite happy to adopt a hands-off role.

However, during the transitional year, the Scottish Office ministerial team changed. The new Scottish Secretary, Michael Forsyth, has a hawkish record on local government, and whilst he appeared to seek a new accommodation with local government, he also returned to the attack on Scottish spending levels compared with England, as a means of defending the Scottish financial settlement. Whilst his predecessor had adopted a 'hands-off' approach on the issue of internal management, Forsyth's team attacked the structures of local councils as top heavy, with too many chief officers; too many highly paid officers (£42k per annum plus); too much variation in numbers and salary levels; and too many administrative staff.[25] The local authority association, COSLA, responded that there had been a reduction of 600 senior management posts.

Utilising the £42k salary figure on which Ministers based their criterion for defining 'senior management', Table 5 below shows the numbers employed in Scotland's new councils. We do, of course, recognise that salary is merely an indicator of employee position. As one Chief Executive told us, 'We look good using this as a cut-off point, as we have large numbers of staff on £40–£41k pa!' In addition, some authorities' figures may represent this desire to attract high quality staff. This kind of analysis is distorted by simple comparisons made for political purposes. However, senior managers are only the tip of the organisational iceberg and the scope for savings in administration depends on decisions about administrative requirements in the round.

Whilst in ministerial rhetoric there was praise for councils adopting 'lean and mean' structures, it is clear that these are the exception rather than the rule. A handful of authorities experimented with structural changes such as executive directors and cognate departments. This certainly in some authorities (for example, Fife, Clackmannan) had the effect of reducing the number of directorates. The key measure, however, is that of senior management numbers, and here we find that, as expected, numbers employed increased with the size of authority. We have excluded the three islands authorities from our analysis as these had existing organisational arrangements.

For analytical purposes we grouped authorities into three categories – large (>300,000), medium (100–300,000) and small (<100,000). Whilst this reveals modest differences in the average number of directorates, it also shows substantial differences in the average number of senior staff between the three categories. There are of course exceptions to the general trend in each category, but these *are* exceptions. The general picture of a strong link between population size and senior staff is what we would expect, and directly related to the volume of work.

TABLE 5
SCOTLAND'S NEW UNITARY COUNCILS SENIOR MANAGEMENT*

Authority	Population (1,000)	Directors	Senior Staff (£42k +)
Group 1 >300,000			
Glasgow	623	18	65
Edinburgh	443	10	54
Fife	352	3	74*
North Lanarkshire	326	9	38
South LanArkshire	307	14	39
Average	*410*	*11*	*54*
Group 2 100,000–300,000			
Aberdeen	219	12	15
Aberdeenshire	226	12	19
Angus	111	13	28
Borders	105	9	13
Dumfries	148	7	45
Dundee	151	9	32
East Ayrshire	123	9	27
East Dumbarton	110	7	22
Falkirk	142	9	35
Highland	207	13	24
North Ayrshire	139	7	21
Perth & Kinross	132	13	15
Renfrew	177	9	29
South Ayrshire	114	7	24
West Lothian	148	5	18
Average	*150*	*9*	*24*
Group 3 <100,000			
Argyll	91	12	13
Clackmannan	49	5	14
Dumbarton	97	9	13
East Lothian	87	5	11
Eeast Renfrew	87	7	23
Inverclyde	89	11	18
Midlothian	80	6	11
Moray	87	4	8
Stirling	82	7	12
Average	*83*	*7*	*14*

Note: * Fife has disputed this figure

Source: Local Government Chronicle

We do not find this surprising. Some of the advocates of management reform in local government may well have been driven by a desire for 'lean and mean' structures, but others are just as concerned with shifting the balance of organisational power to the centre of the authority. This is not uncommon in cases of radical organisational change, as Pollitt's[26] work on the NHS shows. However, in most cases where departments have been amalgamated in the new authorities, in the main this results from the demands of scale other than organisational philosophy. As Black recently observed, 'more continuity than change has been evident. The majority of councils have stuck to what they know best – traditional structures and chief executives'.[27]

Councils in practice still retain the dominant role in service delivery, despite the enabling rhetoric. Moreover, we would argue that there is no *a priori* reason for expecting councils which enthusiastically adopt the enabling model to have leaner structures. Purchaser/provider splits increased bureaucracy in the NHS, and the preliminary evidence suggests little difference in local government. One recent review argued that 'splits had not gone far in undermining traditional departmental boundaries, and while more emphasis was being put on strategic management, there were still major issues about how strategy related to everyday service delivery'.[28] The management role may change in an enabling authority, but that does not of itself require less managers. Indeed, the increasing emphasis on monitoring and control may well require more.

EMERGING ISSUES IN SCOTTISH LOCAL GOVERNMENT

Decentralisation

As the transition from two-tier to unitary status has been taking place, other issues have emerged in the agenda of local politics in Scotland. One issue arising directly from the reorganisation is the question of decentralisation within the new councils. Under the Scottish Local Government Etc. Act (1994), all of the 29 new councils were required to submit a draft decentralisation scheme to the Secretary of State for Scotland by April 1997. Councils' approaches to decentralisation have been by no means uniform. Authorities such as Highland and Fife adopted schemes from day one, retaining the district council boundaries as the units of decentralisation. Others, such as Stirling and South Lanarkshire, engaged in comprehensive consultation exercises as they designed their decentralisation schemes.

The schemes themselves reflect managerial, political and financial decentralisation within the councils. At this stage it is largely services rather than any significant degree of power or influence which has been decentralised. However, the drafts of many councils have reflected aspirations to be much more radical and try to engage local communities using new participatory devices. Fife council has set up a Citizenship Commission and local democracy seminars to engage their local citizenry, and has experimented with citizen juries. Other councils are initiating similar innovative schemes. In the coming years we would expect more councils to do likewise as they seek to heighten their profile as new bodies and endeavour to implement their decentralisation schemes. While, to date, the rationale for decentralisation has been dominated by managerial considerations, there is increasing evidence that local democratic participatory considerations are informing at least part of the rationale of the decentralisation drafts.[29]

Patronage Politics

Most of the new councils in Scotland are Labour-controlled. However, although electorally successful, the Labour Party in Scotland has not been without its troubles. Accusations of sleaze, 'jobs for the boys' and 'votes for trips' have been widespread. This issue emerged during the transitional period but has lingered and still has resonance over two years after the election of the new councils. A wide variety of authorities have faced allegations of improper practice, accusations of sectarianism, nepotism and patronage have appeared in the media. The 1997 Report of the Staff Commission, reviewing appointment procedures, called for 'a more professional approach to the business of appointing senior officers'.[30] Such activities attracted the attention of the Nolan Committee on Standards in Public Life, which recently heard two days of evidence on how to 'clean up' Scotland's councils.

More recently, during Glasgow's recent budget negotiations, Glasgow's Labour leader, Bob Gould stormed out of a meeting of Glasgow's ruling Labour Group after a row with colleagues concerning how to deal with under-funding. After failing to win a vote within the ruling Labour group, he was reported as commenting that some of his colleagues had offered him their vote in return for trips abroad. This has led to an internal party investigation.

These activities may well be manifestations of the dominance of the Labour Party within council chambers – in Glasgow 77 of the 82 members are Labour. A 'factional culture' develops within these councils in which councillors, lacking effective opposition, engage in endless in-fighting over control of key positions with opposing factions emerging within the party. The instability of political leadership has been further exacerbated with the marriage of ex-district and ex-regional councillors, who have, in many

instances, been used to radically different working practices. This problem
is not unique to Glasgow. It is an issue which has to be addressed in many
of the new councils.

Funding

Another on-going problem in the new councils is that of funding. The
'junketing' issue, emerging when it did, largely overshadowed Glasgow's
underlying budgetary problem. Glasgow in April 1997 recorded the largest
council tax increase at 22 per cent. With fewer than one in three of its
citizens earning enough to pay council tax and a shrinking population
Glasgow's budgetary problems are unlikely to disappear. In Scotland
overall council tax levels for 1997/98 rose at more than three times the rate
of inflation, the average increase being 10.7 per cent – compared with
around six per cent south of the border.

Despite large council tax increases, few hold their local council
responsible. Opinion polls have shown that it is the councils which are
winning the propaganda war with the Scottish Office as to who should be
held accountable for the tax increases. An ICM survey conducted just prior
to this year's budgets were set showed 69 per cent blamed the government
for them, with only 24 per cent blaming the councils themselves.[31] At
present the Scottish Office limits how much councils can spend, provides 87
per cent of income and decides how grant is distributed. It would appear,
therefore, that the public have an accurate perception of where the source of
the funding problem lies.

In the first three years of the new councils special transitional
arrangements have been set up, which allow those councils gaining most
from reorganisation to subsidise the losers. The losers are Glasgow,
Dundee, Argyll and Bute, Aberdeen and Midlothian. Before reorganisation
each was part of a regional authority, which could target resources into areas
of greatest social need. As their budgets have been disaggregated, their
grant has been distributed throughout their former area, with obvious
consequences.

The funding issue is unlikely to go away. By committing itself, at least
in its initial two years, to work within the budgetary guidelines already
specified by the Conservatives, Labour is ignoring the major funding
difficulties already apparent. With education, health, housing and industry
identified as Labour's priorities it is difficult not to conclude that the
forthcoming years will see 'more of the same' for councils. These priorities
account for over 60 per cent of total Scottish Office expenditure. Given the
commitment not to increase tax rates or overall public expenditure, then
other expenditures such as roads and transport, environment, law and order

and social work will have to be cut. The Shadow Scottish Secretary admitted 'that there is no pot of gold waiting to be thrown at Scotland's councils'.[32]

Devolution

Although it would appear that little will change in terms of finance, the Labour General Election victory may signal potential constitutional change in Scotland. When devolution was being discussed 20 years ago, the consensus then was that the setting up of an Assembly would inevitably lead to a re-examination of the role of local authorities. There is no reason to believe that this position will have changed. Local councillors are likely to make up a significant proportion of the politicians in a Scottish Parliament, and given that local authority expenditure accounts for 40 per cent of all public spending in Scotland it will inevitably attract attention.[33] It is likely it will do so in the context of a review of the widely perceived 'democratic deficit', with the role of quangos such as local enterprise companies, the water and sewerage authorities and transport authorities coming under review.

In terms of predicting the effects of a Scottish Parliament, we are very much in the realm of conjecture. However, one thing is certain. If implemented, a Scottish Parliament, elected under a proportional representation system, will change the political landscape in which Scottish local councils operate.

CONCLUSIONS

The reorganisation of local government in Scotland was defended by the argument that it would create a more local, more efficient and more accountable system. The vague commitment to decentralisation in itself undermines the rationale for unitary authorities based on boundaries which reflect community identity. Some authorities have simply based their decentralisation scheme along the former district boundaries. We also find it difficult to accept Michael Forsyth's argument that 'the whole ethos of the 1994 Act is to give the new councils freedom to draw up strategies, develop policies, explore solutions',[34] when restrictions on financial and organisational autonomy in terms of the capping and competitive tendering requirements remain.

The *process* of implementation was successful. Staff have been transferred, and services have continued to be delivered with little adverse comment in the media. This is because, as with the poll tax, implementing officials in both central and local government effected reforms successfully irrespective of their disagreement with the principles underpinning them.

Local political actors in the implementation process were more concerned to design organisations to meet their needs than to achieve any efficiency targets claimed for the system by the government.

It is unlikely there will now follow a period of consolidation. Labour, in response to calls from the Convention of Scottish Local Authorities (COSLA) during the election campaign announced plans to launch a major inquiry into the relationship between local councils and central government in Scotland.

As well as looking at the broad question of relations between the devolved Parliament and local authorities it is anticipated that this review will look into matters such as the Scottish spending differential which have been consistently highlighted by Conservative Ministers in Scotland. Ministers have claimed that Scottish councils spend 30 per cent more than their counterparts in England. COSLA has countered this, pointing out that when Scotland's unique characteristics – a higher proportion of children attending state schools, teacher training and qualification system, length of roads maintained by councils, climate, population sparsity, levels of poverty and deprivation, different capital financing arrangements and accounting mechanisms – are taken into account the difference is defensible. As a Scottish Parliament establishes its relationship with Westminster and Whitehall this debate is likely to attract a wider audience.

In conclusion, this paper has sought to question some of the assumptions underpinning local government reform. It has analysed the process of transition, arguing that it has been relatively smooth. The reform process for Scottish local councils is, however, by no means complete, with many new emerging issues now coming into focus.

NOTES

1. G. Boyne, G. Jordan and M. McVicar, *Local Government Reform: A Review of the Process in Scotland and Wales* (London: LGC Communications, 1994).
2. Scottish Office, *The Structure of Local Government in Scotland: The Case for Change* (Edinburgh, 1991).
3. Scottish Office, *Shaping the New Councils* (Edinburgh, 1992).
4. For examples see Adam Smith Institute, *Shedding a Tier* (London, 1989), and Scottish Conservative Unionist Association, *Report of the Working Party into the Reform of Local Government* (Edinburgh, 1992).
5. Boyne, Jordan and McVicar, *Local Government Reform*, p.22.
6. Scottish Office, *Shaping The Future – The New Councils* (Edinburgh, 1993), p.8.
7. Ibid., p.3.
8. Labour Party Scottish Council, *The Future of Local Government in Scotland: A Policy Document* (Glasgow, 1990), p.9.
9. Wheatley, *Report of the Royal Commission on Local Government in Scotland* (Edinburgh: HMSO, 1969).
10. K. Young, 'Attitudes to Local Government', in the Widdicombe Report Research Vol.111, *The Local Government Election* (Cmnd 9800, London: HMSO, 1986).

11. S. Bristow, 'The Criteria for Local Government Reorganisation and Local Authority Autonomy', *Policy and Politics*, Vol.5, No.2 (1977), pp.143–62.
12. M. Chisholm, 'Some Lessons from the Review of Local Government in England', *Regional Studies*, Vol.29, No.6 (1995), p.560.
13. See R. Dahl and E. Tufte, *Size and Democracy* (OUP, 1974); and K. Newton, 'Community Performance in Britain', *Current Sociology*, Vol.22, No.1 (1974), pp.49–88.
14. Boyne, Jordan and McVicar, *Local Government Reform*.
15. S. Black, *The Internal Management of Scottish Local Government* (University of Edinburgh, 1995).
16. J. Stanyer, *Understanding Local Government* (Fontana, 1980), p.8.
17. For example, see R. Kerley and K. Orr, 'Joint Arrangements in Scotland', *Local Government Studies*, Vol.3, No.19 (1993), pp.309–18; Boyne, Jordan and McVicar, *Local Government Reform*; and A. Alexander and K. Orr, 'The Reform of Scottish Local Government', *Public Money and Management* (Jan.–March 1994), pp.33–8.
18. S. Leach *et al.*, *After Abolition: The Operation of the Post 1986 Metropolitan Government System in England* (Birmingham, 1992), p.5.
19. Scottish Office, *Shaping the Future – The New Councils* (Edinburgh, 1993).
20. See, for example, R. McQuaid, 'Costing Local Government Reform', *Local Government Studies*, Vol.19, No.4 (1993), pp.477–486; and A. Midwinter, 'The Review of Local Government in Scotland – A Critical Perspective', *Local Government Studies*, Vol.18, No.2 (1992), pp.44–54.
21. Local Government Staff Commission (Scotland) Annual Report (Edinburgh, 1997).
22. Midwinter, 'The Review of Local Government in Scotland', pp.44–54.
23. A. Midwinter and N. McGarvey, 'The Reformed System of Local Government Finance in Scotland', *Policy and Politics*, Vol.25, No.2 (1997), pp.143–52.
24. Society of Local Authority Chief Executives (Scottish Branch), *The New Management Agenda* (Stirling, 1994).
25. Black, 'The Internal Management of Scottish Local Government'.
26. C. Pollitt, *Managerialism and Public Services* (Oxford: Blackwell, 1993).
27. Black, 'The Internal Management of Scottish Local Government', p.16.
28. V. Lowndes *et al.*, 'New Management, Citizenship and Institutional Change', paper prepared for the ESRC Local Governance Conference, Exeter, 20–21 Sept. 1995, p.5.
29. N. McGarvey, 'Unravelling Two Coalitions for Local Governance Reform', in J. Stanyer and G. Stoker (eds.), *Contemporary Political Studies 1997*, Vol. Two (Belfast, 1997), pp.624–35.
30. Local Government Staff Commission (Scotland) Annual Report (Edinburgh, 1997).
31. *Scotsman*, 28 Jan. 1997.
32. Scottish Labour press release, 24 Jan. 1997.
33. A. Midwinter, 'Local Government in a Devolved Scotland', *Scottish Affairs*, Vol.18 (1997), pp.24–35.
34. Scottish Office, *A Guide to Decentralisation* (Edinburgh, not dated).

The Local Government Review –
An Inept Process

JOHN SINNOTT

INTRODUCTION

As many English local authorities come to terms with their new responsibilities and scarce resources following reorganisation, there is a temptation not to look back at the local government review and the activities of the Local Government Commission. However, to do so would be to draw a veil over some sorry events, and that would be a disservice to local government and its future well-being.

This article looks at the local government review mainly from the perspective of Leicestershire, where the process and the implementation of the recommended changes appear to have been more troublesome than in many other parts of the country. The article considers in a local context the wider dissatisfaction with the review process and the performance of the Local Government Commission, and points to a link between the inadequacies of the review and the subsequent problems of implementation. The conclusion is that the review initiated by the government in 1991, supported in large measure by the opposition parties, was the wrong way to review or to reorganise anything, let alone democratic institutions and public services. The next reorganisation, though perhaps delayed by the national parties' uneasy reaction to this recent review, must be handled differently. Lessons should be learnt, both by those promoting and those undertaking any further reorganisation, and it is noted that the Local Government Commission is still in office.

THE REVIEW PROCESS – SOME GENERAL OBSERVATIONS

Before the local government review of Leicestershire began, the Chief Executive of the Local Government Commission, Martin Easteal, visited the county council. His visit was no more than a courtesy call. He advised that he would not be seen again in Leicestershire; his staff would be in touch

---

John Sinnott is the Chief Executive of Leicestershire County Council

about the 'straightforward' way in which the review would be conducted and would like some basic information on the county; they would visit for no more than a day to familiarise themselves with the area and then get on with that review, and others. It was very much 'thank you and goodbye'.

From that beginning a rigorous process was not anticipated, and it certainly did not materialise. It was also hard not to believe that those undertaking the review, a mixture of part-timers and secondees, wanted the whole process done and out of the way as quickly as possible. Indeed, when in September 1993 the Secretary of State announced an acceleration of the review (to be concluded by December 1994) it was welcomed by the Commission.[1] As a contrast with the Redcliffe-Maud Commission,[2] which remains the last thorough review of local government structure in England, what was on offer from the Banham Commission could not have been more marked. There was a feeling of something at best superficial, with most of the conclusions pre-determined. Banham's public criticism of the 1960s Royal Commission was somewhat at odds with the later references to Redcliffe-Maud in the Local Government Commission's March 1995 report.[3] However, the paucity of debate in the Banham era was reason enough to return to Redcliffe-Maud and Senior,[4] and to find, not surprisingly, that they do repay a re-reading, the changing world of local government notwithstanding.

When the Local Government Commission reported its draft recommendations, the lack of rigour was reinforced. The arguments against the way in which the Commission operated are familiar, but there were three particular criticisms which stood out from the common introduction to the draft recommendation reports. First, the case for unitary authorities was based on assertion; no supporting evidence was adduced. This was at best disappointing, given that the case for unitary authorities was being pushed by government to the centre of the job which the Commission, claiming independence, had been given. Only at the end of the process, with Parliament having decided on structural change, was the point publicly recognised from within, by Professor Michael Clarke, a recruit to the Local Government Commission in June 1995: 'Lastly, right up to the end, the process of review suffered from there having been inadequate general debate about the concept of the *unitary* authority ... Conviction and mere assertion are no substitute for reasoned argument and judgement.'[5] Second, it was hard to see how local accountability could be improved, as claimed, by a reduction in the number of locally elected representatives. The Commission later responded to this concern by addressing it in terms of councillor workload, and remained silent regarding accountability. Third, whilst every independent observer stated that reorganisation would cost money rather than save it, the best the Commission could put forward was the possibility of distant savings. As a cost:benefit analysis, even the framework analysis given in the government's policy guidance to the Commission, the examination script would have failed. Within Leicestershire County Council the review was soon branded as 'intellectually bankrupt', by the Leader of the Liberal Democrat Group, Professor Robert Pritchard, a distinguished academic. That indictment was never bettered.

Looking back to reports which appeared three or four years ago, it is even harder now to relate the timidity of much of the Local Government Commission's written output to the declarations of Sir John Banham. Hubris was the only weapon to hand and it was displayed in force. Banham was fond of recalling his experience with the Audit Commission and the experience of his chief executive with the National Audit Office, to underline their commitment to a review which stood up to scrutiny. His case was unconvincing and, as the whole process brought forth more and more legal argument, it became clear that the real test for the Commission's reports was avoiding the possibility of a successful judicial review application.

In the Leicestershire review, one particularly controversial issue could have been the possible extension of the Leicester boundary. The City Council wished not to see the issue raised, whereas the surrounding district councils were fearful and the County Council, whilst opposed to an extension, considered that the issue was relevant to a debate on the best local government structure for Leicestershire. The following sentence from the draft recommendations report is a neat illustration of how the Commission sought to ensure that it could not be criticised or challenged for avoiding a relevant issue: 'In considering the City's case for unitary status, we have given *some thought* (the author's italics) to whether its boundary should be extended to include parts of adjoining districts.'[6] Three short paragraphs later, no one could say that the Commission had not taken a relevant issue into account. Whether it had done it justice is an altogether different matter, but presumably the Commission thought it had. In a later report, the Commission claimed that 'some thought' amounted to 'detailed consideration'.[7]

Although much of the argument about how the Commission went about its business concentrated on the different versions of the policy guidance set out by the government,[8] significantly changed by the courts at the instigation of Derbyshire and Lancashire County Councils in 1994, the basic terms of reference for the review were the requirements of the Local Government Act 1992, for the Commission to have regard to the need: '(a) to reflect the identities and interests of local communities; and (b) to secure effective and convenient local government.'[9] To start a review from a base position which was potentially confusing and open to different interpretation and opinion was a fundamental mistake. The tensions between the wording of the Act and the direction of the policy guidance were at the heart of a policy and administrative confusion. It led the Commission to come to its recommendations on the basis of opinion polling and consultation, although in the time available any other defensible means of operation was unlikely. Whilst consultation was inevitably open to manipulation and local abuse, opinion polling too was often imperfect. In Leicestershire the inadequacies of this approach were seen in the Commission's refusal to consider and consult on a no-change option, and in the Commission's refusal to take into account in its final deliberations a MORI opinion poll commissioned by the County Council.

'NO CHANGE' AS AN OPTION

In a letter of 10 June 1994 Sir John Banham said:

> In many larger counties in population terms one of the options will be for a continuation of the existing two-tier structure which has often received a wide measure of local support. However, the Commission does believe it right to recognise the capacity of many of the larger former county boroughs to become unitary authorities in their own right, even when the structure in the rest of the county is unchanged.[10]

Although Banham referred to capacity rather than capability, there was a strong indication of special treatment for the pre-1974 county boroughs, but no indication of whether their track record of achievement was deserving. There was also a suggestion of a *return* to county boroughs, ignoring the differences in local government's responsibilities and status then and now. County boroughs might have claimed self-sufficiency, but *unitary* authorities could never make that claim.

Also on 10 June 1994, the lead commissioner for the Leicestershire review, David Thomas, said: 'there are advantages in the existing structure which, on balance, the Commission feels should be retained, except that the very special claims of the City of Leicester and of Rutland should be recognised.'[11] If it was not clear before, it was then obvious that cards had been marked. What was aggravating was the deliberate choice of the Commission to deny, or certainly to frustrate, the people of Leicestershire in not having the opportunity to register their own views on the current two-tier structure as a benchmark. In spite of Sir John Banham seeming to give an assurance at a press conference (also on 10 June) that the no-change option would be included as a tick-box on the Commission's household leaflet, it was not. The Commission was pleased to rely on the judgment in a case brought by North Yorkshire County Council that the Commission was not obliged to include a no-change option on the household leaflet. At the same time, the threat of the Treasury Solicitor was brought to bear on local authorities keen to challenge a refusal which was an unpleasant mixture of arrogance and cowardice.

Leicestershire County Council was unable to obtain an answer or justification from the Commission as to its refusal to offer the no-change option, beyond a terse reference to the Treasury Solicitor's letter. However, as a further indication of pre-determined conclusions, the following appeared in a newspaper advertisement placed by the Commission: 'The Commission's draft recommendation, and the other structural options which the Commission has identified as being potentially viable for your area, are summarised alongside.'[12] By implication, the no-change option was excluded because the Commission did not regard it as a viable option.

In some other areas the no-change option was included in the Commission's household leaflet. In late 1994 National Opinion Polls Ltd (NOP) analysed responses (the bulk of which came in the form of household leaflet replies) on structural change in 22 review areas, of which five had no change as an option. For the areas of Kent, Lancashire, Oxfordshire, Surrey and Warwickshire, household support for no change was measured at 67 per cent, 60 per cent, 70 per cent, 77 per cent and 76 per cent respectively. Were those five areas the only areas where the Commission regarded no change as a viable option, and, if so, why? Why was Lancashire with four cities or boroughs in excess of 120,000 population not then deemed suitable for unitary authorities? Many other similar questions could be put. Whatever the rights or wrongs, the whys and the wherefores, the whole process was flawed with so many anomalies that it became easy to see why the government, particularly in the shape of David Curry, later decided to do something about it. Curry was, of course, looking at a mess of his government's own making. However, to change the policy guidance to the Commission, only for a key part to be struck out by the courts (the Derbyshire and Lancashire case), was making a bad job worse.

Table 1 takes some of the data from the NOP analysis and compares support for the no-change option in descending order in the Commission's recommendations on the 22 areas. The five areas where no change was an option on the household leaflet head the table. Comparably higher levels of support may have been evident through other forms of consultation, but it is interesting to speculate on how much extra support for no change would have been gained in areas with substantial support for no change but which had that option deliberately excluded from the household leaflets. The areas of Cumbria, West Sussex, Cheshire, Cambridgeshire, Nottinghamshire and Leicestershire certainly come into that category. To a degree, the

TABLE 1
SUPPORT FOR OPTIONS

County	No Change (%)	LGC Options			Details of LGC Options	LGC Draft Recommendation	LGC Final Recommendation	Second Review LGC Final Recommendation	Final Result
		Option 1 (%)	Option 2 (%)	Option 3 (%)					
Surrey*	77	19	77	-	1 = 5 unitaries 2 = No change	5 unitaries	No change	No change	No change
Warwickshire*	76	20	76	-	1 = 2 unitaries 2 = No change	2 unitaries	No change	-	No change
Oxfordshire*	70	17	7	70	1 = 3 unitaries 2 = 1 unitary 3 = No change	3 unitaries	No change	-	No change
Kent*	67	14	11	5	1 = 2 unitaries + 2 tier rest 2 = 7 unitaries 3 = 6 unitaries 4 = No change	2 unitaries + 2 tier rest	No change	1 unitaries + 2 tier rest	1 unitary + 2 tier rest
Lancashire*	60	22	6	60	1 = 8 unitaries 2 = 6 unitaries 3 = No change	8 unitaries	No change	2 unitaries + 2 tier rest	2 unitaries + 2 tier rest
Cumbria	53	16	15	-	1 = 2 unitaries 2 = 3 unitaries	2 unitaries	No change	-	No change
West Sussex	49	30	7	-	1 = 1 unitary + 2 tier rest 2 = 3 unitaries	1 unitary + 2 tier rest	No change	-	No change
Cheshire	45	18	4	21	1 = 5 unitaries 2 = 5 unitaries 3 = 1 unitary + 2 tier rest	5 unitaries	No change	2 unitaries + 2 tier rest	2 unitaries + 2 tier rest
Cambridgeshire	38	23	14	14	1 = 3 unitaries 2 = 2 unitaries 3 = 4 unitaries	3 unitaries	No change	1 unitary + 2 tier rest	1 unitary + 2 tier rest

TABLE 1
(CONTINUED)

County	No Change (%)	LGC Options			Details of LGC Options	LGC Draft Recommendation	LGC Final Recommendation	Second Review LGC Final Recommendation	Final Result
		Option 1 (%)	Option 2 (%)	Option 3 (%)					
Nottinghamshire	38	23	11	19	1 = 1 unitary + 2-tier rest 2 = 4 unitaries 3 = 7 unitaries	1 unitary + 2 tier rest	1 unitary + 2 tier rest	1 unitary + 2 tier rest	1 unitary + 2 tier rest
Leicestershire	34	35	14	10	1 = 2 unitaries + 2 tier rest 2 = 1 unitary + 2 tier rest 3 = 5 unitaries	2 unitaries + 2 tier rest	2 unitaries + 2 tier rest	-	2 unitaries + 2 tier rest
East Sussex	23	15	34	-	1 = 4 unitaries 2 = 2 unitaries + 2 tier rest	4 unitaries	1 unitary + 2 tier rest	-	1 unitary + 2 tier rest
Essex	15	53	7	2	1 = 2 unitaries + 2 tier rest 2 = 6 unitaries 3 = 7 unitaries	2 unitaries + 2 tier rest	1 unitary + 2 tier rest	2 unitaries + 2 tier rest	2 unitaries + 2 tier rest
Dorset	14	35	37	-	1 = 3 unitaries 2 = 4 unitaries	3 unitaries	4 unitaries	-	2 unitaries + 2 tier rest
Berkshire	12	18	8	-	1 = 4 unitaries 2 = 4 unitaries	4 unitaries	5 unitaries	-	6 unitaries
Hampshire	11	50	24	-	1 = 2 unitaries + 2 tier rest 2 = 7 unitaries	2 unitaries + tier rest	3 unitaries + 2 tier rest	-	2 unitaries + 2 tier rest
Staffordshire	10	45	7	15	1 = 1 unitary + 2 tier rest 2 = 3 unitaries 3 = 5 unitaries	1 unitary + 2 tier rest	1 unitary + 2 tier rest	-	1 unitary + 2 tier rest

TABLE I
(CONTINUED)

County	No Change (%)	LGC Options			Details of LGC Options	LGC Draft Recommendation	LGC Final Recommendation	Second Review LGC Final Recommendation	Final Result
		Option 1 (%)	Option 2 (%)	Option 3 (%)					
Buckinghamshire	4	27	45	16	1 = 3 unitaries 2 = 4 unitaries 3 = 1 unitary + 2 tier rest	3 unitaries	4 unitaries	-	1 unitary + 2 tier rest
Bedfordshire	3	19	55	17	1 = 2 unitary + 2 unitaries 3 = 2 unitaries	2 unitaries	3 unitaries	-	1 unitary +s 2 tier rest
Wiltshire	3	33	60	-	1 = 3 unitaries 2 = 1 unitary + 2 tier rest	1 unitary – 2 tier rest	2 unitaries + 2 tier rest	2 unitaries +2 tier rest	2 unitaries + 2 tier rest
Hereford and Worcester	2	18	16	59	1 = 3 unitaries 2 = 2 unitaries 3 = 1 unitary = 2 tier rest	3 unitaries	1 unitary + 2 tier rest	-	1 unitary + 2 tier rest
						3 unitaries	1 unitary + 2 tier rest	-	1 unitary + 2 tier rest

Notes :

(i) Figures are taken from the Commission's final recommendations reports for each area. Figures represent responses primarily from the household leaflet returns, but also include letters from individuals and responses from organisations and local interest groups.
(ii) In its final recommendations for Leicestershire the Commission said that it gave more weight to its Stage 3 MORI survey than to these public consultation responses. This was the MORI survey (MORI B) commissioned by the Commission - the results of the MORI survey (MORI A) commissioned by the County Council were ignored.

To bolster its argument for change, the Commission aggregated the responses to the options which included a unitary Leicester. MORI itself acknowledged that such aggregation was 'feasible' but advised that 'such combinations should always be treated with caution, as it may be that respondents' preferences are at least partly based on what would happen outside the district in which they live.' (as reported in the Commission's Final Recommendations on Leicestershire, p.47).

Source: NOP Analysis and Tabulations 1994.

Commission's household leaflets promoted the structural options presented therein to the exclusion of others.

As a postscript it is interesting to note that Surrey, Kent and Lancashire were amongst those areas subject to a further review on the instruction of the government. It would appear that public consultation was more important in some areas than others. As a process, the local government review was not only lacking in consistency but lacking in integrity.

WAS PUBLIC OPINION PROPERLY TAKEN INTO ACCOUNT?

Although no change was not given as a specific option, 33 per cent of Leicestershire residents returned the Commission's household leaflet marked in favour of no change. 36 per cent were in favour of the option for a unitary Leicester, unitary Rutland and two-tier elsewhere. Although the return rate was very low at 2.4 per cent, the County Council was encouraged to believe that its own instinctive views about the strength of feeling in Leicestershire were fairly accurate and continued to press for the debate to be kept informed. Much to the annoyance of the Local Government Commission, the County Council commissioned MORI to undertake an opinion poll immediately ahead of the Commission's Stage 3 research, also to be undertaken by MORI. The County Council had seen drafts of the Commission's Stage 3 MORI survey questionnaire and anticipated (correctly, as it turned out) that the Commission's MORI poll would neither permit the residents of Rutland to choose directly the option of no change nor allow them to weigh the costs of change against no change. The County Council was grateful to MORI in having no hesitation in carrying out the work and seeing no conflict of interest. For convenience, the two polls are referred to here as MORI A (for the County Council)[13] and MORI B (for the Commission).[14] The County Council was concerned to ensure that MORI A was asking questions which put cost and service considerations to the fore.

Table 2 shows the findings from the various stages of public consultation during the Leicestershire review. The data in Table 2 has been arranged roughly in chronological order, although, because of the overlap in the various surveys, it is impossible to be sure if this sequence is a valid chronology. The absence of a level of support which would have justified change of the eventual magnitude is apparent, although it is difficult to make proper comparisons between the different sets of data. This is partly because of the exclusion of no change as an option in the household survey and the Commission's Stage 3 research, and also partly because of the large percentage of 'don't knows' in each of the MORI surveys. The main points to emerge from the comparative analysis are that Leicester residents increasingly did not know their preferred option for a local government

TABLE 2
RESPONSES TO PUBLIC CONSULTATION IN LEICESTERSHIRE

Responses to Public Consultation in the Local Government Review of Leicestershire

In favour (%)	Commission's Household Leaflet				Household Leaflet plus individual letters sent to Commission			
	O	DR	L	R	O	DR	L	R
No change	33	48–22	37	9	34	49–23	39	10
Unitary Leicester, Unitary Rutland, 2-tier elsewhere	36	38–24	38	62	35	36–22	37	60
Don't know	—	—	—	—	—	—	—	—

	MORI A June–July 1994 (%)				MORI B July–August 1994 (%)			
	O	DR	L	R	O	DR	L	R
No change	47	66–39	42	21	21	40–11	17	12
Unitary Leicester,	11	18–6	9	46	15	23–5	14	34
Unitary Rutland, 2-tier elsewhere	15	17–7	21	17	26	39–12	36	15

O = Overall
DR = District range (excluding Leicester and Rutland)
L = Leicester
R = Rutland

structure, that support for a unitary Leicester declined steeply in the later polling, and that support for a unitary Rutland declined throughout. This was hardly an endorsement of change.

The Rutland case for change rested entirely on the strength of community identity. In 1993 a MORI survey[15] had shown in respect of Rutland residents that 80 per cent indicated a very or fairly strong feeling of belonging to Rutland. However, in the same survey only 19 per cent of Rutland residents thought that a sense of local community was one of the three most important factors in deciding local government structures. By far the most important factors were quality of services, responding to local people's wishes and cost of services, measured at 74 per cent, 61 per cent and 39 per cent respectively. The debate on Rutland should have been about balancing the emotional feelings with the rational side of argument. Although the Commission identified the likely costs to the taxpayers of change, the proper balance to the argument was never achieved, hard though the County Council tried.

In its final report, the Commission suggested that the people of Rutland understood the cost of unitary status.[16] Presumably that view was based on the Commission's household leaflet, which, albeit in small type and without emphasis, set out the estimated cost of change (an additional £83–£125 per Rutland household each year) and the same leaflet being shown to people being interviewed by MORI in August 1994. In MORI B people had the opportunity to say whether cost was a factor in their structural preference, but no specific cost questions were asked. Table 3, however, shows the increasing concern of Rutland residents about cost and its relative importance amongst factors in determining local government structure. The table also shows that, whilst 36 per cent were prepared to pay more (for a unitary authority), only 31 per cent of those were prepared to pay more than £50 extra in council tax. This was a very clear message: almost 90 per cent of Rutland residents were not prepared to pay anything like the cost from their pockets that the Commission warned would be the price of a unitary Rutland. The findings of MORI A were available to the Commission and yet it still went ahead with its recommendation for change.

SOME CONCLUDING THOUGHTS AND LESSONS

The outcome of the Leicestershire review is a structure which, on the Commission's own estimates, will produce extra annual costs of £1–£6 million, and transitional costs of £4–£6 million, never to be paid back. The effect on the council tax for 1997/98 is shown in Figure 1. A more realistic figure for the transitional costs comes from the supplementary credit

TABLE 3
RUTLAND RESIDENTS' VIEWS ON THE IMPORTANCE OF COST AND OTHER FACTORS

	* MORI (1993) Rutland residents (%)	MORI A (1994) Rutland residents (%)
'From this card, which three of these, if any, do you think should be most important in deciding the local government structure in your area?'		
Ease of contacting the council	22	12
Historical or traditional boundaries	18	14
Cost of services	39	62
Quality of services	74	74
Level of information provided by the council about its services	15	22
Ease of access to local Councillors	15	9
Responding to local people's wishes	61	61
Sense of local community	19	20
Size of population covered	6	7
Location of council offices	12	8
Other	–	1
Don't know	3	2

	* MORI (1993) Rutland residents (%)	MORI A (1994) Rutland residents (%)
'Would you be prepared to pay more for your local services to cover the cost of any change in structure?'		
Yes		36
No		55
Don't know		9
[Asked only of those prepared to pay more] *'How much extra in council tax would you be prepared to pay?'*		
Up to £50		49
£51 to £100		28
More than £100		3
Don't know		20

Note: *MORI (1993) = Research Study into Community Identity.

Source: MORI

approvals received by the three affected authorities over 1996/97 and 1997/98, a total of £10.5 million, with each authority admitting that the approvals are insufficient to cover its costs. In the City of Leicester, cuts in services from April 1997 have had to be introduced on a scale not previously seen, whilst the council tax has significantly decreased.

FIGURE 1
1997/98 COUNCIL TAX

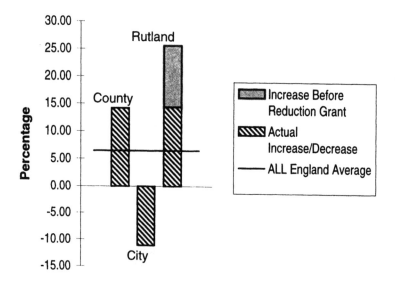

At the same time, the benefits of reorganisation have still not been quantified beyond general assertions. Whilst the final sentence of paragraph 3 of the government's policy guidance may have been struck out by Mr Justice Jowett in January 1994, the first sentence remained: 'Unitary authorities can reduce bureaucracy and costs and improve the co-ordination and quality of services.'[17] A claim could equally have been made that the local government review would increase bureaucracy, add to costs, weaken the strategic planning of services and reduce the quality of services through a reduction in resources. The sadness of the local government review was that the Commission embarked upon its task with no attempt to reconcile these competing claims. After three years' work, the Commission's inability or unwillingness to identify the case for unitary local government had not advanced, as witnessed by four brief paragraphs within the 150 pages of the

Banham Commission's valedictory report.[18] The government's policy guidance (June 1995 version) brazenly claimed that the Commission's report had expanded on the case for unitary local government.[19] The truth was that the case had not been argued through and the Commission was found wanting in not demonstrating the intellectual rigour and honesty which would have enabled an independent body to challenge the compromising task it had been given. It is revealing to learn subsequently of the criticisms of the process made by one commissioner, Professor Chisholm.[20]

In the early summer of 1997 is there anyone who would not argue that a reorganisation of local government could have been handled better. Whatever the outcome, change or no change, there were more acceptable ways, managerially and professionally, never mind politically, of getting there. So how did the local government review come about, and what lessons are there for the future?

First, there is a need for realism. The local government review was adversarial and there is simply no denying the fact. Those who claim otherwise ignore the nature of the review, and also the stuff of politics. Leicestershire County Council was criticised by Leicester City and Rutland Councils for its opposition to the review, sometimes forgetting that the County Council met its statutory obligations about information and co-operation. There were really no grounds for criticism given that the County Council was able to demonstrate the weakness of the Commission's methodology. The County Council was entitled to maintain its opposition to the review – after all, Leicester and Rutland were not backward with their opposition to the 1974 changes, and the effect of reorganisation on the continuing County Council was underestimated by the proponents of change. Politics will never be excluded from reorganisation but this review was almost designed to provoke disagreement.

The terms of reference for any future review must be clearly understood, the range of options clearly identified and not subject to external or internal manipulation. In reality, all that is needed is a return to the normal way of working for any independent commission established by government on the principle of consensus. However, in the case of local government, there should be a prior consideration – that is, a decision on its role and functions, embracing the revenue and capital funding regimes. In the early days of the review, weasel words emerged from the Commission about the value of its work whilst divorced from the debate (such as it was) about local government's role, financing and management.[21] Later, it was particularly disappointing to see, within an evidently more thoughtful approach to review, the Local Government Commission under Sir David Cooksey's chairmanship writing in its September 1995 report:

whilst the Commission is properly concerned with the establishment of councils which are viable in resource terms, it cannot concern itself with the wider criticisms of local government about the "equity" of annual revenue support grant negotiations. And yet, this issue regularly sought to invade the Commission's task.[22]

To those who have sought to defend the institution of local government, the last sentence is almost offensive. It detracts sharply from the generally favourable reception accorded to the Commission under Cooksey's chairmanship when, acting with a restricted brief, it undertook a further review, in isolation, of 21 districts. If those Commissioners saw themselves as making the best of a bad job, as was commonly believed in some cases, then it should not have been beyond them to have drawn attention to the strait-jacket of their terms of reference rather than treat it as a cocoon. Whether or not the Commissioners carry on in office, there is an absolute need for an informed parliamentary debate on what local government is and should be about before any further review is undertaken. There is no point in designing a structure without knowing its purpose.

Secondly, local government needs to help itself. Those who argued for reorganisation in the late 1980s and early 1990s, often arrogantly, only succeeded in dividing much of local government. Never again should local government consent to a structural review with so much potential for internal damage. There is a very considerable task here for the new Local Government Association, particularly if there is an attempt to rekindle the review by one or two disenchanted district councils, let alone the consequences of the emerging debate about regional government. If local government is unable within itself to come to a measured and mature position on, say, what constitutes *strategic* and what defines *community* – where the Local Government Commission arguably failed – then the future is not optimistic. The answers to these questions, it is noted, often reveal the necessity of a multi-tiered approach.

Thirdly, the interests of staff need better consideration. The local government review has seen the jobs and careers of thousands of staff bedevilled by uncertainty or worse. Local government has lost a wealth of experience, through enforced retirement in many cases. The impact of the Staff Commission[23] has been negligible and local government has been rightly scornful of that Commission's unwillingness to troubleshoot or to act as an honest broker. In any future reorganisation, local government should be allowed to set its own staffing regulations, within its own accustomed rules, and be afforded a meaningful dialogue with central government about the cost implications.

Fourthly, the legal framework for the review was hopelessly inadequate.

As commented above, the statutory terms of reference pointed towards confusion, but the back-up regulations compounded the problem, failing to cater for the common hybrid outcome of a mixture of two-tier and unitary authorities within a single review area. There was a stubborn refusal by the legislators to treat all reorganising authorities the same, particularly as regards shadow elections, until people almost ceased to care which was a new and which a continuing authority. The implementation of reorganisation before some authorities had been elected was bizarre and but one example of avoidable problems which Whitehall and Westminster effectively passed on to local authorities. Perhaps next time the promised approach of collaboration will pay dividends and Whitehall will actively seek the views of those who have to implement government policy. Certainly the pretence of *consultation* on draft regulations and guidance, with ridiculous turn-round times, which characterised the local government review, should never be repeated.

Finally, there is the question of methodology. Can we look again, as this article has tried to do, at how the Local Government Commission set about its business, and for the future introduce rational argument in place of dubious and selective opinion polls and a form of consultation which was really a licence for the Commission to print its own conclusions. If the Commission post-Banham went some way to introduce a more consistent set of considerations, then the introduction of the 'centrality' concept,[24] for instance, only brought an even greater element of subjectivity into the review exercise. Such was the methodology employed that the conclusions were not so much a matter of balance as of opinions.

A civil servant worn down by the local government review once commented that 'there have to be unitaries somewhere'. In the past tense that remark encapsulates the sham that was the review. It was, after all, what the policy guidance, perhaps the real villain of the piece, drove the Commission to do. Those of us involved recognised the likely outcome only too well, but did we have to endure an exercise where *no national blueprint* became an excuse for a range of different conclusions rather than a desirable objective? It deserved to be opposed. The local government review was an inept process, shameless as much as shameful. Even the poll tax produced an admission of error. If not now, when will the local government review produce the same? If the lessons are not learnt, the only loser will be local government itself.

NOTES

The views expressed are the personal opinion of someone who was on the receiving end of the local government review. They do not necessarily represent the views of Leicestershire County Council, although it is worth noting that all the political groups represented on the County Council from 1989 to 1993 and from 1993 to 1997 were opposed to the process of the local government review, though not to the possibility of reorganisation if a legitimate case could be proved. The review of Leicestershire did not substantiate such a case.

The author would like to thank Ian Malley for his help in assembling information from various opinion poll sources.

1. Local Government Commission for England, *Local Government Review – Procedural Advice on the Preparation of Proposals* (November 1993), p.2.
2. Lord Redcliffe-Maud (Chairman), Royal Commission on Local Government in England, 1966–1969, Volume I, Report, Cmnd. 4040 (London: HMSO).
3. Local Government Commission for England, *Renewing Local Government in the English Shires – A Report on the 1992–1995 Structural Review* (London: HMSO, March 1995), pp.16–22.
4. Royal Commission on Local Government, op. cit., Volume II, Memorandum of Dissent.
5. M. Clarke, 'A Poisoned Chalice? The Re-constituted Local Government Commission', *Public Administration*, Vol.75 (Spring 1997), pp.109–18.
6. Local Government Commission for England, *Draft Recommendations – The Future Local Government of Leicestershire* (London: HMSO, June 1994), p.19.
7. Local Government Commission for England, *Final Recommendations on the Future Local Government of Leicestershire – A report to the Secretary of State for the Environment* (London: HMSO, Dec. 1994), p.31.
8. Department of the Environment, *Policy Guidance to the Local Government Commission for England*, first issued July 1992, revised November 1993, further revised June 1995.
9. Local Government Act 1992, Part II, S.13(5).
10. Letter from Chairman of the Local Government Commission for England to certain local authority chief executives, 10 June 1994.
11. Local Government Commission for England news release, 10 June 1994.
12. Local Government Commission for England newspaper advertisement, referred to in Local Government Commission, *Final Recommendations on Leicestershire*, p.13.
13. MORI Research Study, June–July 1994, *Leicestershire Residents Survey 1994.*
14. MORI Research Study, July–Aug. 1994, *Leicestershire Stage 3 Research.*
15. MORI Research Study, May–June 1993, *Community Identity in Leicestershire.*
16. Local Government Commission, *Final Recommendations on Leicestershire*, p.29.
17. Department of the Environment, *Policy Guidance*, November 1993 revision.
18. Local Government Commission, *Reviewing Local Government in the English Shires*, pp.16, 18.
19. Department of the Environment, *Policy Guidance*, June 1995 revision.
20. See 'Who said size was not important?', *The Independent*, 4 Oct. 1995; and M. Chisholm, 'Some Lessons from the Review of Local Government in England', *Regional Studies*, Vol.29, No.6 (1995), pp.563–9; 'Independence under Stress', *Public Administration*, Vol.75 (Spring 1997), pp.97–107.
21. See, for example, Local Government Commission for England, 'Renewing Local Government in the English Shires – A Progress Report' (London: HMSO, Dec. 1993), p.2.
22. Local Government Commission for England, *The 1995 Review of 21 Districts in England* (London: HMSO, Sept. 1995), p.5.
23. The Local Government Staff Commission (England) was established in May 1993 under s.23 of the Local Government Act 1992. Guidance to the Commission was issued by the government in June 1993. As with the Local Government Commission, the Staff Commission was affected by broad terms of reference, backed by restrictive guidance.
24. Local Government Commission for England, *The 1995 Review*, pp.19–20.

LGR: A Bizarre Can of Worms

TIM MOBBS

It is hardly necessary to recount now the bizarre changes in directions and guidance provided by central government. The July 1993 guidance, although not binding on the Commission, made it clear that, though 'in some areas the Commission may wish to recommend the continuation of the existing two tier structure', central government expected that to be the exception. I could not have been the only unitary council employee to have shifted to the shires to help extend unitary councils to the countryside. But the guidance was challenged in the courts. Ultimately, towards the end of the process, even the Minister in charge was publicly telling audiences across the country that there would be no change in most of rural England. But he did not stop the process. He allowed councillors, officers, pressure groups, voluntary associations, the media and the public to become embroiled in a costly farce which left nothing but anguish and bad feeling where previously a reasonable harmony had existed.

Also bizarre was the timetable. The measured pace of the original plan for the English reorganisation contrasted sharply with those in Scotland and Wales. The Commission's brief was to assemble evidence – something thought unnecessary in the other countries. Because it was an evidential process, the project was to have been tackled in 'tranches'. That way some learning could have happened. Had the process been a disaster, or if unitary authorities in rural areas could be seen to be a mistake, it could have been aborted in many areas without negative result.

The way arguments were assembled and dismantled with scant regard to the evidence by people of whom we were entitled to expect more was equally bizarre. Of course we expected each tier to be partisan. What was more surprising was the partisan nature of the academic input into the debate. Those, like Stewart and Jones (who had always argued for the strengthening of local government) sought to undermine the proponents of the unitary authority. Of course they were correct to point out that the unitary nature of the London boroughs and metropolitan districts had proved no panacea. Of course they were right to remind us that there was no such thing as a 'most purpose authority', since there were a plethora of

Tim Mobbs, South Norfolk District Council

quangos vying with the local authorities for pre-eminence in particular fields in the locality. But what they failed to express was the need (if local government was to mean anything) for a single clear voice to speak out for the citizens of the area.

The academic advocates of local government had long criticised the way the Heath government had overridden the planned Redcliffe-Maud report of 1969 on the grounds that unitary authorities that were large enough for some services would be too large for others. Stewart had, for example, honestly pointed out the folly of justifying a particular size of authority on the basis that size was necessary to sustain 'a specialist music adviser post'. The pattern which emerged in 1974 contained such variation that it could rightly be said that almost any pattern of local government could deliver services.

Though central government may not always share this view, since the universal franchise the key responsibilities of local government have been:

- the reconciliation of competing interests and the building of community cohesion;
- the articulation and government of difference;
- the exercise of countervailing power against over centralised national government.

Given this, why undermine those who sought to construct the mechanism that could best serve such a purposes?

The Local Government Commission paid MORI to study community identity in considerable depth. They seemed surprised to discover the obvious fact that community identity is not a simple matter. It was hardly a surprise to those of us in rural areas that identity was strongest with the local village or neighbourhood. Local government in many Western countries is organised on that basis. But it was clear that central government had no real wish to empower the parishes in more than a token way. In my view, this emphasis on community *identity* was misplaced. The delineation of community *interest* would have been more relevant.

This preoccupation with 'affective' rather than 'effective' community merely reinforced the case for multi-tier local government – and could even have been used to justify a regional upper tier. But the way the LGR drama was played out in rural counties provided all the evidence that anyone could need to show that the three-tier system of local government is a recipe for conflict and confusion rather than the means to build consensus in the community. Of course, there will always be differences in view between localities, and between region, county, district and parish scale. But the strength of the unitary authority relies on its capacity to listen to and *reconcile* these perspectives, rather than *amplify* them, with the ultimate effect that central government is asked to arbitrate, as it is when planning applications are 'called in', or even solving the parish pump politics of local commons. As MORI has since argued, people are more concerned with results than process. If the problem is to manage the complexities of linked urban and rural economies and systems then unitary authorities are the answer as much in the late 1990s as they were in the late 1960s.

The Redcliffe-Maud Committee had taken this as read. The only argument for them was size. The majority report advocated large unitary councils because this would usually enable the retention of the emotionally important counties (though in the case of Norfolk, a large part of Suffolk was to be appended). The minority report had stressed a different argument, based less on emotion and 'affect' than lifestyle and 'effect'. Both agreed that the daily routine of the economy and society of cities like Norwich, York or Gloucester clearly extended beyond their tightly drawn boundaries, though the minority report suggested for Norfolk a central unitary council based on Norwich which extended from the coast beyond the Suffolk border. On the east coast, a unitary combining Great Yarmouth with Lowestoft and their respective rural hinterlands described a socio-economic reality which transcended historical and emotional boundaries. Those changes were not implemented. For reasons which had more to do with nurturing grassroots support for the Conservative Party, the three-tier system was retained in 1974.

It was therefore ironic, bizarre even, that it was a Conservative central government which justified the mid-1990s reorganisation on grounds that it would address 'the extent to which dissatisfaction remains with the local outcome of the last reorganisation in 1974'. When MORI conducted the first round of public opinion surveys for the 1990s reorganisation, they found all over the country popular support for the *idea* of unitary councils.

Game has argued that that there was 'incontrovertible evidence of the slippage between people's majority support for the principle of unitary authorities in Stage 1 community identity surveys and the distinct lack of enthusiasm for specific unitary structures'.[1] He depicts that as evidence of lack of support for change – and certainly 40 per cent of those who felt strongly enough to write to the Commission were in favour of no change. But the unitary options considered in most counties (Rutland being the exception) were for large authorities with about 200,000 population. In rural areas, like Norfolk, that meant authorities with very large spatial extent.

The fascinating, and very positive, aspect of the local government review was the opportunity it gave us all to rethink what local government was for. Across the country two million people expressed their views. It offered those of us on the inside a chance to stop, think and argue for what we really wanted local government to be like. In our case, in South Norfolk, we consulted our citizens, employing NOP to carry out a systematic market research. People were asked first about principles, then about five specific structure options, and then asked again after being told about the costs. Again it showed that more than 60 per cent of our citizens wanted unitary authorities – but it also showed that two-thirds wanted councils to cover *smaller* areas, separating the city from the more rural areas (see Figure 1A). The preference for a small, rural, unitary South Norfolk was only slightly reduced when the issue of costs was introduced (see Figure 1B).

The early indications given by the Commission that it wanted any new structure to cost no more than the existing one, and therefore it wanted unitary authorities in 150,000 to 250,000 population bands, forced the advocates to formulate proposals which merged district councils. In Norfolk, for example, there was an early consensus that four districts should merge, reducing their number from seven to five. But even at that scale the county and its supporters made great play with the capacity of such organisations to support specialist staff.

FIGURE 1

CITIZENS' PREFERENCES FOR LOCAL GOVERNMENT IN SOUTH NORFOLK

A: FIRST AND SECOND CHOICES BEFORE CONSIDERING COSTS

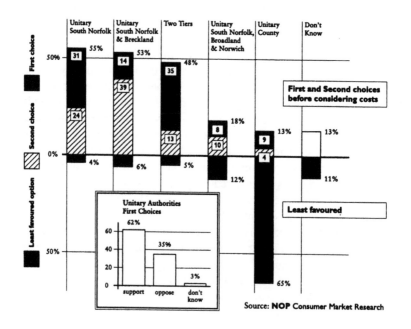

Source: **NOP** Consumer Market Research

B: FIRST AND SECOND CHOICES AFTER CONSIDERING COSTS

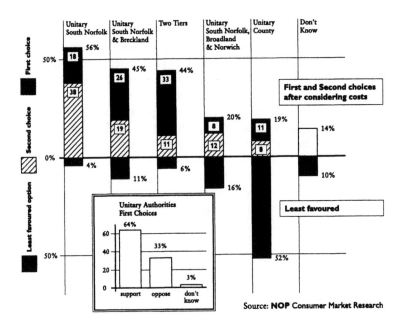

Source: **NOP** Consumer Market Research

It was particularly bizarre that in a decade when 'partnership' tripped off every politician's tongue, the notion of joint arrangements was actively discouraged by the Commission. So facile attempts were made to show that these merged district unitaries were big enough to cope with everything. In fact, of course, no local authority could be self-sufficient, nor should it ever try to be. The 1990s was the decade of 'contracting out', of 'compulsory competitive tendering', and of the 'purchaser/provider split'. If this was Conservative policy, what better way to secure it than to create unitary districts so small that they *had* to buy services from provider units. The provider units could have been organised at whatever scale was most efficient for the provision of services. There would be no need for them to fit a county or district of a given size or with particular emotional significance.

My council was the first in Norfolk to drop out of the consensus on big merged unitaries. The majority of members of the hung council argued that a district that was 50 miles from end to end was little better than a county that was 80 miles across. Having worked hard to develop and promote our case for change, my colleagues and I were understandably dismayed by our members' decision. But in retrospect perhaps they were right. The bizarre constraints imposed by the Commission had forced us to promote a size of unitary which was *too big* to capture popular support, and if this happened in Norfolk it was probably true across rural England. This explains the 'slippage' between concept and concrete proposals.

We shall probably never know whether my analysis is correct, because it would certainly be bizarre if the new central government hurried to reopen such a can of worms as the LGR. But Warren Hatter tells me that the data that MORI gathered is not inconsistent with my view.

The Conservatives seem to have comprehensively reorganised themselves out of Scotland and Wales, where they made little attempt to consult the public before imposing a pattern of 'big' unitaries, and now control none of them. Of course, their recent lack of success in the general election was not wholly attributable to the bizarre LGR, and in fact at county level they have done marginally better in the *status quo* districts than in 1993. Far be it that I should imply an element of gerrymandering in those areas where Labour and Liberal unitaries have been carved out of otherwise predominantly Tory counties, but I think the message should now be clear that a reorganisation inspired mainly by a malign intent 'to get even' with or destroy councils like Derbyshire and Cleveland which insisted on exercising their countervailing power is not a sound basis on which to reorganise.

Let us hope that next time it is done better, with fewer preconceptions and a more open mind. But let us also hope that, eventually, there *will be* a next time, for a system of three-tier local government, in which each tier is structured to challenge the others, is not serving local people well. The case for three separate tiers has been over-played. If an issue as local and minor as a village common needs the involvement of three tiers of local government but still has to be referred to central government for final approval, there must be a case for a change in the law in that area at least. But the separation of housing from social services, of the youth service from community leisure, and of waste collection and recycling from waste disposal all illustrate the outdated view that responsibility must be tied to service delivery. For six or seven years we need to monitor closely the successes and failures of the few unitaries with small populations that have now been created and see then if there is a case to reopen the can of worms.

NOTES

This paper is written from the perspective of an officer who was involved actively in the abortive efforts to reorganise local government in a predominantly rural county. From that perspective it certainly was a bizarre process.

1. Chris Game, 'How Many, When, Where and How? Taking Stock of Local Government Reorganisation', *Local Government Policy*, Vol.23, No.4 (1997), p.7.

Local Government Reform in the US – And Why it Differs so Greatly from Britain

DONALD F. NORRIS

The recent Local Government Review in Britain has prompted considerable attention to the subject of local government reorganisation by scholars and government officials in Britain. For good or ill, local government reorganisation or reform today rarely attracts attention, scholarly or otherwise, in the United States. Yet it is possible, even likely, that an understanding of one nation's experience of local government reform may be valuable to another, especially when important issues of local government structure and function are at stake.

The purpose of this paper is to examine local government reform in the US, to explain why it differs so greatly from that of Britain, and to draw some conclusions about the implications of local government reform in the US for Britain. In so doing, I will focus on three periods of American history in which significant changes in the structure of local government either occurred or were attempted.

The US and Britain operate within distinct constitutional, legal, historical and cultural frameworks. This is another way of saying that, regardless of many similarities, there are also significant differences between the two nations. Among other things, these differences are revealed in the structure and functioning of their respective local governments. They also affect the ways in which reforms to local government structure and functions occur in both countries.

LOCAL GOVERNMENT REORGANISATION IN BRITAIN

Four major local government reorganisations have occurred in Britain in the past 35 years. These were: (1) in 1965, when the Greater London Council and the 32 London boroughs were established; (2) in 1974, when the overall number of local governments was reduced, many local governments, especially those in metropolitan areas, were consolidated, new local government boundaries were drawn, and six metropolitan counties were established; (3) in 1986, when the Greater London Council and the six

Donald F. Norris, University of Maryland, Baltimore County

metropolitan counties were abolished; and (4) the recently concluded Local Government Review which, although adding a few new unitary authorities, resulted in only modest changes to the structure of local government in Britain.

To an American observer, perhaps the single most important characteristic of these reforms of local government in Britain is that they were initiated and carried out by central government. In Britain, the central government, through its majority in Parliament, is supreme when it comes to the structure and functions of local government. Hence, it can change local government structure and those functions almost at will.

This characteristic is also perhaps the biggest single difference between the British and American political systems in general and the way that those systems address local government in particular. Local government reform in the US cannot proceed at the behest of the federal government. Under the American Constitution, the federal government has no direct role in local government. This is a province reserved exclusively to the states. Indeed, local government is not even mentioned in the Constitution.

Because local government, and hence local government organisation and reorganisation, are matters exclusively reserved to each of the 50 states, when it occurs at all, local government reform tends to move slowly and unevenly across the political geography of the nation. For this, among other reasons, local government reform is also much more difficult to achieve in the US than in the UK.

LOCAL GOVERNMENT REFORM IN THE US

The US has witnessed three periods in its history during which local government reform has occurred or been attempted. In two of those periods considerable reform occurred, while in the third considerable effort produced few substantive results. Those periods were the era of Jacksonian democracy, the Age of Reform and the period of metropolitan reform.

Era of Jacksonian Democracy[1]

According to Adrian and Press, the era of Jacksonian democracy witnessed the ascension of the politics of the common man throughout the American political system. They argued that the basic tenets of American local government ideology, which began with Thomas Jefferson, were fundamentally transformed under Jacksonian democracy.[2] Jefferson was largely responsible for articulating the concept of local autonomy, especially the autonomy of the citizen in his local government. However, Jefferson's theory was both elitist and anti-urban in the sense that it was derived from the autonomy of the landed gentry living in small self-governing rural communities. Moreover, Jefferson himself and his followers were highly suspicious of cities and their urban hordes.[3]

Jefferson's notion of local autonomy was modified by Jacksonian democracy 'which provided a rationalisation for city government that survived nearly intact for the remainder of the nineteenth century and is still important in our thinking today'.[4] The fundamental principles of Jacksonian democracy were: (1) 'government by the common man' – or the notion that every man was as qualified as any other to hold office, hence, there should be no qualifications (such as property ownership) for holding office; (2) 'universal manhood suffrage' – which eventually led to voting rights for all citizens; (3) elected rather than appointed office – to make office holders accountable directly to the people, which led to the creation of a large number of elected offices in American local governments.[5] By the beginning of the Civil War, the principles of Jacksonian democracy had taken hold throughout American local government.

Jacksonian democracy also led to 'extreme deconcentration of both legislative and executive responsibilities'.[6] In particular, it saw the rise of use of boards and commissions to operate numerous aspects of city government, fragmenting and decentralising city government policy making and administration. Among other things, this deconcentration and decentralisation opened the door to a variety of abuses of government that, in turn, helped to produce the reform movement, about which I shall have more to say presently.

The changes that occurred in local government structure during the period of Jacksonian democracy were not the result of any formal movement at the local, state or national levels to reform local government. No reform organisations, civic leagues, voters or taxpayers organisations or other such groups rallied citizens to the banner of municipal reform. Nor did state governments actively place local government reform on their agendas. Rather, what seems to have happened is that, during this period, the principles of Jacksonian democracy became widely accepted, and their steady diffusion throughout the nation had dramatic consequences for the structure of local government.

One of these consequences was the considerable weakening of city governments.[7] This weakening came at a time when municipalities were being stretched mightily to meet the basic needs for public works and services of burgeoning populations. In the 30 years between 1840 and 1870, the US population more than doubled from 17 million to 39.8 million, and its urban population more than quintupled from 1.8 million to 9.9 million. The growth of particular cities was even more spectacular. The city of Chicago grew from 4,500 to nearly 300,000; St Louis from 16,000 to 310,000; and New York from 370,000 to 1.5 million. This meant that city governments were faced with the massive task of accommodating an incredible influx of population and for providing the public facilities and services demanded by such population increases. American cities' ability to meet these demands in the late nineteenth century with virtually no state or federal assistance has been labelled by one historian as one of the unheralded triumphs of the cities.[8]

The Urban Machine and the Age of Reform

Although American cities performed nearly Herculean feats in meeting the unprecedented demands of population growth and should be duly credited for so doing, not all that occurred in this period was equally positive. Most of America's larger cities witnessed graft, corruption, fraud and waste, the growth of urban slums, inequities in the delivery of public services, particularly to newly arriving immigrant groups, and crime and violence on a scale never before and not since seen in the nation.

In this setting, in the late 1800s, appeared that unique American institution, the urban political machine.[9] Because they were not especially concerned with the legalities of their behaviour, urban political machines were able to employ extra-legal means to centralise power in an otherwise decentralised or fragmented political environment. By so doing, they were able to control the supply of certain goods, such as municipal jobs, government contracts, and police protection, which could then be delivered to favoured groups, such as ethnic immigrant voters and legitimate and illegitimate businesses for a *quid pro quo* of other values, such as votes, payoffs and kick-backs.

From the late 1800s to roughly the onset of World War II, urban machines (as well as a variety other real and perceived governmental and corporate ills) came under serious and sustained attack in a period that has come to be known as the 'Age of Reform'.[10] The principal focus of the municipal reform movement was to change the structure of local governments in order (it was argued) to prevent the corruption so prevalent under urban machines.[11] The municipal reformers were driven by noble as well as ignoble motives. In reaction to the ills of the cities, they sought to end graft, corruption, vice, scandal and to improve the lot of city dwellers. They also wanted to bring efficiency, economy and professional administration to city affairs and to centralise and strengthen the institutions of city government. Less nobly, the reform movement was xenophobic, anti-immigrant and motivated by exaggerated fears of the working classes and the poor. According to some scholars, the conflict between the reformers and the machines represented a struggle between social classes pitting middle and upper classes WASPS, who perceived a steady erosion of their dominance in civic affairs, against the lower classes, especially ethnic immigrant groups, whose power of the ballot was leading to their political control of city after city through the mechanism of the urban machine.[12]

The principal structural changes sought by the municipal reformers included:

- strong mayor form of government, or, alternatively, the council-manager form of government;
- the use of professionally trained administrators;
- merit-based civil service systems;
- unicameral legislatures;
- voter registration;
- non-partisan, at-large, off-year and off-cycle elections;
- citizen initiative, referendum and recall;
- the adoption of municipal home rule charters; and
- the use of cost accounting principles.

The reformers argued that these structural changes would help to end the corrupt practices of the machines, would prevent their future occurrence, would take local government away from the bosses, would place local government on more of a business-like basis and would make it more efficient.

The municipal reform movement was well-organised, initially at the local and state levels and then nationally. Municipal reform was represented by a number of civic organisations, including taxpayers' leagues, voters' leagues, business groups and other similar organisations in the cities and states and such as the National Municipal League, the League of Women Voters and the Municipal Research Bureau movement. At the national level, reform was most clearly represented by the Progressive political party.[13] These and other organisations carried forth the message of reform from the local to the national level and from one end of the nation to the other.

Although for different reasons and in different ways, the municipal reformers of the late nineteenth and early twentieth centuries had as significant an impact on local government structure in the US as did the principles of Jacksonian democracy in the previous century. Most of the structural reforms that were advocated by the reform movement have long since been adopted in whole or in part in local governments across the United States. Reform structures are particularly evident in local governments in the western United States, in smaller cities and in suburban America. Typically, it is only the largest American cities, especially those in the east and mid-west, many of which had a tradition of machine rule and which even today have the greatest ethnic and other political cleavages, where reformed structures are less frequently present. And even in those cities, at least some of the reformed structures can be found, for example, strong mayor form of government, merit-based civil service systems, home rule charters, cost accounting principles and voter registration.

Metropolitan Reform

Local government reform returned to the American public agenda in the second decade following the end of World War II. From the late 1940s and to the contemporary period, America's urban population has continuously spilled out of the nation's central cities into ever more distant suburbs. At the same time, typical American metropolitan areas have become increasingly fragmented with from tens to hundreds of governments serving them.

For at least the past 35 years, strong evidence has been mounting that shows that uncontrolled metropolitan growth and metropolitan fragmentation have produced serious negative social, economic and environmental consequences.[14] These consequences have included:

- Economic classes and racial groups have become increasingly separated from one another spatially, with central cities and older, inner suburbs housing most of the minority population of metropolitan areas while the newer suburbs are overwhelmingly white.
- Metropolitan areas exhibit great disparities of wealth among local jurisdictions, with most of the poor located in the central city and the older, inner suburbs while the newer suburbs are overwhelmingly affluent.
- Because of the disparities of wealth, metropolitan areas experience equity problems with regard to taxation and levels of public services. That is, there is generally a higher incidence of taxation in poorer jurisdictions, notably but not solely central cities, combined with these jurisdictions' lesser ability to deliver quality public services.
- The cost to extend and maintain public facilities and infrastructure and to provide a wide variety of public services is far greater in a sprawling than a contained urban area.
- Increasing amounts of farm and forest land are being lost to urban development.
- Air and water pollution have increased with the wider distribution of the population over a greater land area.
- Exclusionary zoning and other land use practices are employed by suburban jurisdictions to keep 'undesirable' populations, such as the poor, minority group members and generally the lower socio-economic classes, out of the suburbs (which, in turn, means higher concentrations of these populations into the central cities).

- Central cities subsidise suburban residents, who make daytime use of many central city services and facilities (zoos, parks, sports stadiums, arts and cultural institutions, and so on) without having to pay for them.
- High housing cost and exclusivity in the suburbs forces the poor to the central cities, while the suburbs refuse to allow public or subsidised housing for the poor within their boundaries.
- Local government autonomy means that all jurisdictions are equal when it comes to land use planning and development control. Consequently, development is characterised by a crazy-quilt pattern and jurisdictions actively complete with one another for development.
- It is nearly impossible to co-ordinate services across governmental boundaries. Consequently, there is duplication of services and a loss of economies of scale that might otherwise be possible.
- Finally, there is no governmental official or body that is responsible for the metropolis as a whole. This means that the needs of the parts are attended to (because each part has its own government) but the needs of the entire territory are not.

Suburban sprawl and metropolitan fragmentation have occurred hand in glove in metropolitan America. Sprawl is a function of the urban population increase that has taken place in the absence of systematic, consistent metropolitan-wide land development controls and metropolitan-wide governing structures. The absence of land use and development controls is the result of two important factors. First, Americans believe that land ownership conveys extensive rights, including the nearly unfettered right to develop. Thus, it would be anathema to the American belief in property rights to limit an owner's right to sell or develop land. Even today, ten years after the fall of the Berlin Wall and with it the fall of international Communism, it is not unusual for demands for the regulation of land development in the US to be labelled socialist or Communist.

As difficult as it may be for a British or European reader to fathom, these terms carry very significant negative political meaning in the American context. Indeed, in most parts of the US, proponents of development control often find it necessary to dress their regulations in environmental or other garb (for example, controlling development along river banks is necessary to prevent water pollution) in order to make them even modestly palatable.

A second important factor abetting sprawl is that American local governments rely heavily on the property tax. On average, the property tax makes up about 30 per cent of local government general revenue and about 75 per cent of overall local government revenue. On average, local governments receive about one-third of their total revenues from the federal and state governments.[15] Among other things, this means that American local governments are relatively autonomous when it comes to their finances and, thus, the provision of services. However, the trade-off involved is Damoclean. In order to achieve financial autonomy, local governments must encourage land developments that provide a net revenue surplus to the jurisdiction. Because the amount of development that might occur in any metropolitan area is finite, local governments find that they must compete with one another for desirable developments.

Sprawl is also abetted by a nearly complete absence of areawide land use planning and development regulation in US metropolitan areas. Throughout the US, land use planning and development regulation are almost always the exclusive province of the most local level of government. Additonally, there is no requirement for the myriad local governments to co-operate or co-ordinate with one another in land use planning and development regulation. Consequently, development can and does take place in an unco-ordinated fashion driven both by market forces and by what developers are able to persuade local planners and regulators to permit.

Two significant reasons for metropolitan fragmentation are that, with a few notable exceptions, state governments (1) have made it difficult (some would say impossible) for most central cities to annex territory and population outside their boundaries and (2) have made it relatively easy for suburban residents to incorporate new local governments. Until the years immediately following World War II, annexation had been the primary method by which cities were able to contain urban population. As the urban population expanded beyond city boundaries, cities extended their boundaries to encompass that population. As a result of limits placed on the annexation powers of the central cities and ease of incorporation of suburban governments, older central cities in the US are today largely ringed by autonomous incorporated suburbs.[16]

The negative consequences of sprawl and fragmentation cited earlier served as a justification for the metro reformers to propose new structures for metropolitan governance. The structures most favoured by the metro reformers were those that more closely matched the spatial distribution of the metropolitan population, and, hence, the needs of the population and the territory, with governmental boundaries. In addition, the metro reformers felt that larger governmental units provided a greater possibility of achieving economies of scale. A larger size unit would have a larger resource base, and larger size also meant greater efficiencies in such things as procurement, operation of specialised units, co-ordination of services and facilities, and strategic planning.

The reform structures included: city–county consolidation (in which city and county governments effectively became one), single metropolitan-wide governments, and two-tier and three-tier governments. Less drastic alternatives included strengthening urban county governments, improving formal and informal co-operation among metropolitan jurisdictions, establishing councils of government, and using single and multi-purpose special districts.

Whatever the merits of the case for the metropolitan reform, it has produced very few successes. For example, between 1960 and 1992, only 18 city–county consolidations occurred in the US.[17] Of these, only five occurred in areas that might be said to have had substantial urban populations at the time of consolidation.[18] They were: Nashville–Davidson County, Tennessee (1962); Chesapeake–South Norfolk–Norfolk County, Virginia (1962); Virginia Beach–Princess Anne County, Virginia (1962); Jacksonville–Duvall County, Florida (1967); and Indianapolis–Marion County, Indiana (1969). The remaining 13 consolidations occurred in areas with under 250,000 in population.

In addition, only one two-tier and two three-tier reform structures have been established. And not a single metropolitan-wide government has been established. In 1957, Miami–Dade County (Florida) adopted a two-tier system. Under this system, Dade County is solely responsible for certain county-wide functions and can also set some standards for performance of other functions by the constituent jurisdictions of the county. Three-tier reform structures have been adopted in the Portland, Oregon, area by a vote of the people in 1978, and in the Minneapolis, Minnesota, area by an act of the Minnesota state legislature in 1969. In both of these cases, however, the area-wide organisation (which sits atop both city and county governments) has limited functions and authority. Moreover, in all three cases there has been considerable controversy at one time or another and their success in addressing metropolitan-wide needs has been limited.[19]

FACTORS CONSTRAINING LOCAL GOVERNMENT REFORM IN THE UNITED STATES

This review of local government reform in America leaves two important questions unanswered. Why has local government reform not happened more frequently in the US? And why has metropolitan reform failed when local government reform occurred across the nation during the era of Jacksonian democracy and in the Age of Reform? I would suggest at least the following reasons: (1) America's written federal Constitution; (2) the status of local governments in state constitutions; (3) state political tradition; (4) American local government ideology; (5) local government autonomy; and, finally, (6) the strength of contemporary pro-sprawl, pro-fragmentation forces.

Federal Constitution

As noted earlier, the federal Constitution does not permit the national government a direct role with regard to local government. Yet the nation's history does admit of three exceptions. First, during periods prior to statehood in what were then federal territories, the federal government provided for complete governmental control, including local government.[20] However, once statehood was granted, control over local government became the responsibility of the state. Second, in the years immediately after the Civil War, the federal government essentially controlled all state and local government in the occupied southern states. Finally, in periods of national emergency such as in the aftermath of hurricanes, floods, or urban riots, if a state government should so request, the President may dispatch federal troops or nationalise state national guard units to provide assistance and law enforcement within state and local jurisdictions. Except in these cases, however, the federal government has no direct role in America's 83,000-plus local governments. Among other things, this means that efforts to reform local government must be initiated at either the state or local level.

Local Government Status in State Constitutions

State constitutions typically contain numerous provisions guaranteeing the status of local governments and their officials. For example, the state constitutions often contain provisions for the existence, structure and functions of local governments and for the existence and functions of certain local elected officers. Consequently, American local governments possess both constitutional and legal status. Importantly also, local governments are granted specific, and in many cases exclusive, territory by constitutional or legal provisions. Thus, both inertia and the interests that grow up around local government structure and functions operate heavily in favour of the *status quo*, making it difficult to reform American local governments.

State Political Tradition

Historically, American state governments have been reluctant to meddle in the affairs of local governments.[21] In part, this is because of the American local government ideology, about which I shall have more to say presently. In part, this is a recognition that, as a Speaker of the US House of Representatives once quipped: 'All politics is local.' State legislators and governors tend to leave as much decision making as possible at the local level because legislators especially must run for re-election in local districts. Indeed, many state-level politicians began in politics as local elected officials and proudly proclaim that they did. They are not inclined in the first instance to challenge the prerogatives of local governments. Moreover, if their actions in the state capitol were perceived as being antithetical to local government, they might be challenged in the next election by local elected officials or voted out of office by the citizens of their districts.[22]

Periodically, of course, neither of these powerful forces is sufficient to keep state governments from becoming directly involved in local affairs. However, it usually takes a crisis or near crisis for this to happen.[23] Berman estimates, for example, that at least 20 US municipal school districts have been taken over by their states since 1989. These include the states of Illinois, New Jersey and Ohio, which have taken over the local public school systems of the cities of East St. Louis, Newark and Cleveland, respectively. Additionally, the states of Massachusetts and New York have essentially taken over (at one time or another) significant features of the local government of the cities of Chelsea and New York. The fact remains, however, that states rarely involve themselves directly in the affairs of local governments.

Local Government Ideology

Americans believe that the closer a government is to the citizens (that is, the more local it is), the more likely it will be to serve the citizens well. Conversely, the more remote a government is (for example, state or federal government), the less likely it will be to do so. This belief is much more than a civics book lesson or election year rhetoric. It is deeply held, especially at the local level. The ideology can be traced to the theories of Thomas Jefferson concerning the sovereignty and autonomy of the individual in his local community.

Local government ideology has contemporary significance as well. For example, public opinion polls routinely show that American's rate their local governments higher than either state or federal governments. Moreover, the ideology is actually practised at the local level, as will be seen in the discussion of local government autonomy below.

Local Government Autonomy

As Syed has pointed out, early American settlers believed that sovereignty should be:

> diffused to the point of ultimate residence in the individual himself. ... They adopted certain governmental forms and rejected others according as these accommodated or repelled their fundamental assumptions in political philosophy. Thus, they gave their units of local government a considerable measure of autonomy. With the passage of time, the philosophy behind the practice of local autonomy

acquired the status of a myth.[24]

While the influence of this theory 'among serious students of local government would appear to have all but vanished'[25] and its constitutional basis is non-existent, the theory of local autonomy remains a powerful received truth in American politics.

Americans widely believe that their local government ought to be autonomous, especially in certain critical areas of life.[26] Of equal importance, no matter how flawed it may be in theory, local autonomy is widely practised by American local governments. State constitutions give citizens broad rights to establish and modify their local governments. Few local governments are ever abolished, and few local units or local functions are taken over by state governments.

Local governments possess considerable discretion in the types of services they provide, the levels at which the services are provided and the manner of their provision. They have considerable discretion in local taxation. And, finally, local governments have considerable discretion in the way they spend their revenues. Thus, although local governments are legally creatures of their states, local governments nevertheless possess and exercise considerable autonomy. Moreover, they are generally treated by state governments as if they were autonomous.

Danielson observes that local autonomy provides local governments, especially suburban governments, with important power over housing and land use functions.[27] Moreover, he argues that: 'In most metropolitan areas, the mozaic of small and independent suburban jurisdictions has foreclosed comprehensive planning, areawide controls on development, and regional instrumentalities empowered to regulate and conserve land, water, and other natural resources.'[28]

Who then would reform or reorganise local governments in America? The federal government has no constitutional role. State governments do not like to become involved in matters that are thought best left to local citizens. Thus, reform, if it is to come at all, must come from the local governments themselves. Because they are relatively autonomous, American local governments cannot be forced to co-operate with efforts that might limit their powers or might result in their demise. Naturally, then, they do not. Indeed, local governments almost uniformly oppose reform of any kind , especially that which might involve even the slightest diminution of their power.[29]

Strength of Pro-Sprawl Forces

In the era of Jacksonian democracy and the Age of Reform, unique historical circumstances, the compelling power of reform ideas, and, during the Age of Reform, the strength of pro-reform forces produced local government reform across the nation. In the current period, metropolitan reform has been spectacularly unsuccessful. This is largely because of the power imbalance between the forces advocating reform and those opposing it, the strength of suburban political autonomy, and the weakness of the ideas behind metropolitan reform.

Metropolitan reform has mainly been the province of academics, newspaper editorial writers, land use planners, a few national organisations of limited influence, such as the League of Women Voters and the National Civic League, and a few business organisations such as chambers of commerce and the Committee for Economic Development. None of these groups have strong political bases in local communities. Moreover, their advocacy of metro reform tends to be on the basis of reform as a vague, generalised good to be achieved at some equally vague point in the future.[30]

Aligned against them are myriad groups with strong bases in local communities and strong interests in the immediate outcomes of local decisions, especially in the realm of development. Indeed, their self-interests are best served by maintenance of the current fragmented metropolitan governmental system. Groups that often oppose metropolitan reform include land developers, home builders, commercial developers, real estate sales organisations, suburban residents, suburban elected officials and state elected officials from suburban constituencies. Many observers argue that development interests are especially important in local government land use policies. This, in turn, 'has negated the role of local land use controls in guiding growth and protecting the environment along the metropolitan rim.'[31]

As if this array of supporters of the *status quo* were not enough, metro reform also confronts the reality of suburban political autonomy. Because they are autonomous and because metro reform threatens the *raison d'être* of their existence, suburban governments oppose metropolitan reform. Suburban opposition today is more significant than ever because about 60 percent of the US metropolitan population now resides in the suburbs.

Finally, the very validity of the ideas behind metro reform have been called into question. In the two earlier periods of local government reform in the US, the ideas underpinning local government reform were widely accepted and acted upon by the population. In the period of metropolitan reform, the intellectual basis for reform has been much less widely accepted and hardly acted upon at all. The analyses and recommendations of the metro reformers have been challenged not only by the groups whose self-interests are threatened by reform, but also by academics from the 'public choice' school who claim that the fragmented metropolis is a more efficient mechanism than a metropolitan-wide government would be. During the Presidency of conservative Republican Ronald Reagan, the public choice position was essentially adopted by the federal Advisory Commission on Intergovernmental Relations and received considerable advocacy through various ACIR publications.[32]

As a consequence of these factors, metropolitan reform has had very few successes and numerous failures. Indeed, the Jeffersonian ideology of local government is alive and well. As I have said elsewhere, the American people have shown their preference for governmental arrangements in metropolitan areas and that preference is for a highly fragmented and decentralised governmental system.[33]

Moreover, it does not appear that any of the factors that constrain metropolitan reform will change in the near future. For example, I see no evidence that the federal constitution will be amended to give the federal government a role in local government structure and functions; that state constitutions will be amended to remove protection for local governments; that the tradition of state governments generally respecting local autonomy will be reversed; or that local government ideology or local government autonomy will weaken. Finally, I see no evidence that the balance of forces advocating and opposing metropolitan reform will shift in favour of the remaining metropolitan reform.

IMPLICATIONS FOR BRITAIN

What, if anything, do these findings from local government reform in the US imply for Britain? While it may not be possible to draw direct parallels because of the differences in constitutional, legal, historical and cultural frameworks between the two countries, certain patterns are nevertheless notable. The first is that several actions by the British central government in recent years have increased the amount of fragmentation in urban areas in Britain. These actions have included the abolition of the GLC and the metropolitan counties in 1986, the recent Local Government Review, requirements for compulsory tendering, and the continuing privatisation and quangoisation of local functions.

The type of fragmentation that has occurred is less in the numbers of new general purpose local governments (although the Local Government Review did produce a few additional unitary authorities) than in functional terms. Many services that once were provided by local governments and were considered an integral part of those governments (such as public transport, water supply, refuse disposal, and others) are now provided by joint boards or authorities, private companies or quangos. As Leach and Game have observed, the abolition of the Metropolitan County Councils produced 'somewhat bewildering variety of [local government] institutions'. This, in turn, weakened public accountability and reduced public knowledge and understanding of local government.[34] A second pattern, and one that is being closely watched by local governments and scholars in Britain, is the increased use of special districts and authorities.[35]

To the extent that these patterns continue, they have the potential to produce a local government system in Britain that is increasingly like the local government system in the US. That is, British local government, especially in metropolitan areas, will increasingly feature multiple, competing and overlapping governmental (and non-governmental) organisations that perform functions and provide services for the residents of the area.

If these patterns continue, they may also follow another American trend and produce a strong constituency for a new *status quo*; that is, for greater fragmentation. This constituency would include the governmental organisations and officials and other service providers (for example, joint boards and authorities, quangos, and privatised service delivery organisations) whose existence is a direct result of fragmentation and who, therefore, support it. If the American experience is any guide, such a constituency can have profound negative consequences for future reforms that are of a more rational nature.

A third pattern concerns land use planning and, with it, the control of land development. A central finding from America is that in the absence of area-wide land use planning and development control, urban sprawl cannot be contained. Additionally, the fragmentation of local government combined with local autonomy (especially over land use) have meant that it is impossible to achieve area-wide land use planning and development control.

Should fragmentation continue apace in Britain, it will become increasingly difficult to co-ordinate land use planning and development control. In a research project I recently completed, I found that intergovernmental co-operation in two English conurbations suffered from ' lowest common denominator' phenomenon. That is, intergovernmental co-operation and co-ordination can only occur with the consent of all intergovernmental parties. This essentially means that a single entity (the lowest common denominator) can scuttle co-operation by its opposition or withdrawal of ascent. I also found that individual local governments could successfully pursue developments that were opposed by other local governments and that had negative impacts on the other governments and on the conurbations as a whole.[36]

While the recently completed Local Government Commission did not contribute in a major way to increasing fragmentation in Britain, it nevertheless created some few additional unitary authorities. Perhaps more importantly, it did not address the boundaries of those or other local authorities to make them more consistent with their urban catchment areas. Consequently, land use planning will be made more difficult by the (admittedly small number of) additional unitary authorities and by the failure of authority boundaries to capture their 'natural' territories.

Many British observers will argue that these trends are unhealthy and undesirable. Indeed, they may be, especially since they make area-wide land use planning and development control more difficult, and these have been hallmarks of local government in Britain in the post World War II era. They have also been used quite successfully in containing urban growth.

From the American perspective, however, the situation in Britain is far from grim. To begin with, urban areas in Britain are much less fragmented and far more rationally planned and controlled than in the US. The legal mechanisms and popular and governmental support for urban containment are strong in Britain. Moreover, in the final analysis, the central government through Parliament remains sovereign and can, at will, reform local government. It is the latter, I suspect, which has caused concern in recent years in Britain – not necessarily that central government can undertake to reform local government, but rather the way in which it has gone about local government reform. Here, perhaps, two modest suggestions may be in order.

First, future central governments would do well to learn from the absence of rational and reasonable principles underlying recent local government reorganisations in Britain (especially the 1986 abolition of the GLC and the metropolitan counties and the Local Government Review). My recommendation here would be that rational principles rather then partisan politics and ideological considerations should inform attempts to reform local government in Britain. Second, central government might look towards America for examples of what not to do – namely, not to permit or encourage nearly unrestricted metropolitan sprawl and not to permit or encourage the further fragmentation and decentralisation of metropolitan areas.

The reason for this is simple. If sprawl and fragmentation are permitted in Britain as they have been in the United States, Britain will forego the opportunity to address area-wide problems and issues on an area-wide basis. Britain will also place itself squarely on the path leading to the negative consequences produced by fragmentation and sprawl in American metropolitan areas – a path down which the US has travelled so far that there is now little or no opportunity to return.

NOTES

I should like to thank Dale Thomson for assisting in the search for scholarly works on local government reform in the US for this paper.

1. This era began roughly with Andrew Jackson's election to the presidency in 1828 and continued at least through the years immediately following the Civil War.
2. Charles R. Adrian and Charles Press, *Governing Urban America* (4th edn., New York:

McGraw-Hill, 1972), p.68.

3. Ibid., p.68; and Anwar Syed, *The Political Theory of American Local Government* (New York: Random House, 1966), pp.38–48.

4. Adrian and Press, op. cit., p.69.

5. Ibid., pp.69–70.

6. Ibid., p.71

7. Ibid., pp.70–72.

8. Jon C. Teaford, *The Unheralded Triumphs* (Baltimore: Johns Hopkins University Press, 1984).

9. Merton has argued that the weaknesses of the cities in the late nineteenth century, which were produced partly by the application of the principles of Jacksonian democracy to city governments, enabled urban machines to develop and thrive. (See, Robert K. Merton, *Social Theory and Social Structure* (New York: Free Press, 1957). This view, however, is not without it critics. See, for example, Alan DiGaetano, 'The Rise and Development of Urban Political Machines: An Alternative to Merton's Functional Analysis', *Urban Affairs Quarterly*, Vol.24, No.4 (1988).

10. Richard Hofstadter, *The Age of Reform* (New York: Vintage Books, 1955).

11. The municipal reformers of this era can be divided into 'structural' and 'social' reformers. The former, who strove to reform local government structure, were far more numerous and successful than the latter, who sought to address such issues as poverty, disenfranchisement, big business influence on municipal affairs, and inequity in service delivery. In this paper, my focus is on structural reform.

12. Hofstadter, op. cit., pp.174–86.

13. See, for example, ibid.; and Adrian and Press, op. cit.

14. See, for example, Robert Wood, *Suburbia: Its People and their Politics* (Boston: Houghton-Mifflin, 1958); Scott Greer, *The Emerging City* (New York: Free Press, 1962); Luther Gulick, *The Metropolitan Problem and American Ideas* (New York: Knopf, 1962); US Advisory Council on Intergovernmental Relations, *Urban America and the Federal System* (Washington, DC: US Government Printing Office, 1969); Amos H. Hawley and Basil G. Zimmer, *The Metropolitan Community: Its People and Government* (Beverly Hills, CA: Sage Publications, 1970); and Drew Dolan, 'Local Government Fragmentation: Does It Drive Up The Cost of Government?' *Urban Affairs Quarterly*, Vol.26, No.1 (Sept. 1990).

15. US Bureau of the Census, *Governmental Finances* (Washington, DC: US Government Printing Office, 1993). The average can be misleading. Larger central cities tend to rely more heavily on federal and state funds, while the newer, more affluent suburbs rely more on own-source revenue. County and township governments and school districts rely more heavily on the property tax than do municipalities.

16. See, for example, Harrigan, op. cit., pp.348–50; and Ross and Levine, op. cit., pp.364–8. For one view of the importance of annexation to American cities today, see David Rusk, *Cities Without Suburbs* (Washington, DC: Woodrow Wilson Center Press, 1993).

17. Ross and Levine, op. cit., p.324.

18. Out of over 3,000 counties and over 19,000 municipalities in the US.

19. See, Edward Sofen, *The Miami Metropolitan Experiment* (New York: Anchor-Doubleday, 1966); John J. Harrigan, and William C. Johnson, *Governing the Twin Cities Region: The Metropolitan Council in Comparative Perspective* (Minneapolis, MN: University of Minnesota Press, 1978); Anthony White, 'Portland Merges Regional Agencies', *National Civic Review*, Vol.67, No.7 (1978); Carl Abbott, *Planning Politics and Growth in a Twentieth-Century City* (Lincoln, NE: University of Nebraska Press, 1983); William C. Johnson, and John J. Harrigan, ' Political Stress and Metropolitan Governance: The Twin Cities Experience', *State and Local Government Review*, Vol.19, No.3 (1987); Harrigan, op. cit.; and Ross and Levine, op. cit.

20. This is true today in territories like Puerto Rico, the US Virgin Islands and Guam, and local government in the District of Columbia operates under a grant of authority from Congress.

21. David R. Berman, 'Takeovers of Local Governments: An Overview and Evaluation', *Publius*, 25 (Summer 1995), pp.55–6.

22. I can cite no empirical data or case studies to support my contention here. However, based

on more than 25 years of observing and interviewing state and local government officials in
several states in the US, I am confident that it is accurate.

23. Berman, op. cit., p.56.
24. Syed, op. cit., p.21.
25. Ibid., p.5.
26. Williams distinguishes between lifestyle and systems maintenance issues in which the author
    argues that 'lifestyle issues' (such as education, housing, zoning, police protection) are so
    important to the citizens of the autonomous local governments in metropolitan areas as to
    make it very difficult to achieve metropolitan governance. See, Oliver Williams, 'Lifestyle
    Values and Political Decentralization in Metropolitan Areas', *Southwestern Social Science
    Quarterly*, 48 (1967).
27. Danielson Michael N. Danielson, 'Suburban Autonomy', in Dennis Judd and Paul Kantor
    (eds.), *Enduring Tensions in Urban Politics* (New York: MacMillan Publishing Company,
    1992), p.372. (Originally published in Danielson, *The Politics of Exclusion* (New York:
    Columbia University Press, 1976).
28. Ibid. p.383.
29. See, for example, David K. Hamilton, 'Political Officials and Areawide Government
    Reform', *Urbanism Past and Present*, 8 (Summer 1979).
30. In the heyday of metropolitan reform, several states appointed commissions to review and
    make recommendations about local government structure. The commissions released reports
    that were notable for the similarities in their diagnoses and prescriptions. See Vincent L.
    Marando, and Patricia S. Florestano, 'State Commissions on Local Government: A
    Mechanism for Reform', *State and Local Government Review*, 9 (1977). The commissions'
    reports also were similar in that they led to very little actual reform. This was largely because
    the commissions had no power to compel reform and because the forces of the *status quo*
    were strong enough to prevent reform.
31. Danielson, op. cit., p.383.
32. See, for example, Robert B. Parks, and Ronald J. Oakerson, 'Metropolitan Organization and
    Governance: A Local Public Economy Approach', *Urban Affairs Quarterly*, Vol.25, No.1
    (1989); and Ronald J. Oakerson and Roger B. Parks, 'Metropolitan Organization: St. Louis
    and Allegheny County', *Intergovernmental Perspective* (Summer 1991).
33. Donald F. Norris, 'Killing a Cog: The Death and Resurrection of the Baltimore Regional
    Council of Governments', *Journal of Urban Affairs*, 16 (1994), p.166.
34. Steve Leach and Chris Game, 'English Metropolitan Government Since Abolition: An
    Evaluation of the Abolition of the English Metropolitan County Councils', *Public
    Administration*, 69 (Summer 1991), p.170.
35. Howard Davis and Declan Hall, 'Matching Purpose and Task: The Advantages and
    Disadvantages of Single and Multi-Purpose Bodies' (Birmingham: Institute for Local
    Government Studies, University of Birmingham, 1996).
36. Donald F. Norris, 'The Governance of British Conurbations: Or How British Local
    Authorities Manage the Metropolitan Territory in the Absence of Metropolitan
    Governments' (A paper presented at the 1997 Annual Meeting of the Urban Affairs
    Association, Toronto Canada, April, 1997).

Notes on Contributors

Neil Barnett spent 12 years as a Local Government Officer before becoming an ESRC Management Teaching Fellow at the School of Economics, Policy and Information Analysis at Leeds Metropolitan University. He is researching into local government reorganisation, with particular reference to the concept of community.

George Boyne is a Distinguished Senior Research Fellow in the Public Services Research Unit at Cardiff Business School, University of Wales. His research interests include public choice theory, competition in local government and the determinants of variations in local authority policies and performance.

Howard Davis is a member of the Institute of Local Government Studies at the University of Birmingham. He worked with several local authorities on their local government review activity and has authored a book on the subject. He has also been a key contributor to the QUANGOs debate. Publications include *QUANGOs and Local Government* (Cass, 1996).

Robert Leach is a Principal Lecturer in the School of Economics, Policy and Information Analysis at Leeds Metropolitan University. He has a long-standing research interest in local government reorganisation, and is a joint author of *Local Government and Thatcherism* (Routledge, 1990). He has also written on political ideologies and changes in party political allegiance.

Neil McGarvey is a lecturer in the Department of Government at the University of Strathclyde. His research interests include local democracy and policy making.

Arthur Midwinter is Dean of the Faculty of Arts and Social Sciences at the University of Strathclyde. His main research interest is in local governmet and he was a member of the Local Government Staff Commission from 1994 to 1997.

Tim Mobbs is Head of Central Services at South Norfolk Council. He has experience in County, District and Metropolitan councils and has also worked in social services, economic and community development, housing renewal, strategic management and organisational development, including consultancy for local authorities in Malaysia and Sri Lanka.

Donald F. Norris is Professor of Policy Sciences and Director of the Maryland Institute for Policy Analysis and Reasearch at the University of Maryland Baltimore County (USA). He is a specialist in managerial and urban policy and in the application, uses and effects of information technology in governmental organisations.

John Sinnott is the Chief Executive of Leicestershire County Council, having worked for the authority for ten years. He has been Chief Executive since 1994. Apart from a short spell as a consultant, his previous career was spent in local government in Liverpool and Merseyside, where he lived through the 1986 metropolitan counties reorganisation.

INDEX

Titles of Related Interest

PARLIAMENTS IN WESTERN EUROPE
Now in Paperback
Edited by Philip Norton

With New Preface

This book provides a much needed analysis of the role of parliaments in western Europe. It focuses upon the relationship of parliament to government and - a neglected dimension of parliamentary studies - of parliament to the citizen. When first published in 1990, it quickly established itself as an essential reference work. This reprint includes a new preface by the editor establishing the context in which legislatures are now viewed and the need for study of the existing parliaments of western Europe.

1997 2nd Edition 155 pages
0 7146 4331 9 paper

QUANGOS AND LOCAL GOVERNMENT
A Changing World
Edited by Howard Davis

Recent years have seen a major transformation in the way that local communities are governed. There is now an appointed world of local governance sitting alongside elected local government. Many apppointed bodies (popularly known as QUANGOs) are seen, from the local government perspective, as 'domain intruders' and are often viewed with resentment and suspicion.This book seeks to develop understanding of the changing world of local governance and thus contribute to wider debates. The impact of these changes will continue to be felt for many years to come – whoever is in government.

1996 112 pages
0 7146 4735 7 cloth
0 7146 4324 6 paper

POLITICS IN AUSTRIA
Still a Case of Consociationalism?
Edited by Richard Luther and Wolfgang Müller

This volume analyses changes to the traditional key features of post-war Austrian politics and questions the appropriateness of Austria's continued designation as a consociational political system.

1992 232 pages
0 7146 3461 1 cloth

FINANCING EUROPEAN LOCAL GOVERNMENTS
Edited by John Gibson and Richard Batley

The financing of local governments is a fundamental determinant of their effectiveness and efficiency. This book surveys the systems of finance that have developed in ten European countries. It shows that while they have confronted a similar range of issues, each has tended to develop its own response with little reference to the others, and that internal political forces and struggles play an important part in determining the roles, powers, discretion and finances of local government.

1993   160 pages
0 7146 4513 3 cloth

THE POLITICAL EXECUTIVE
Politicians and Management in European Local Government
Edited by Richard Batley and Adrian Campbell

Whilst considering the principles on which the British collective executive and legislature is based, this book covers a variety of international issues and manifestations of the political executive, including Oslo's experiments in shifting from an aldermanic cabinet system and provides an account of reforms in the relationship between politics and administration in Sweden.

1992 87 pages
0 7146 3480 8 cloth

UNDERSTANDING THE SWEDISH MODEL
Edited by Jan-Erik Lane

1991 210 pages
0 7146 3445 X cloth

POLITICS IN THE NETHERLANDS
How Much Change?
Edited by Hans Daalder and Galen A Irwin

1989 188 pages
0 7146 3361 5 cloth

www.ingramcontent.com/pod-product-compliance
Ingram Content Group UK Ltd.
Pitfield, Milton Keynes, MK11 3LW, UK
UKHW020428010325
455677UK00029B/1060